The Tower and the Glory

THE TOWER AND THE GLORY
THE WADE DOOLEY STORY

WADE DOOLEY
WITH
GERRY GREENBERG

Best Wishes

Wade Dooley

MAINSTREAM
PUBLISHING
EDINBURGH AND LONDON

First published in Great Britain in 1992 by
MAINSTREAM PUBLISHING COMPANY (EDINBURGH) LTD
7 Albany Street
Edinburgh EH1 3UG

ISBN 1 85158 461 7

A catalogue record for this book is available from the British Library

Typeset in Janson by CentraCet, Cambridge

Printed in Great Britain by Butler & Tanner Ltd, Frome

Simply dedicated to you,
Sharon, Sophie and Sara,
the true stars in my life

Contents

Acknowledgments

I USED to believe only top novelists became rich from writing books
but now I'm not so sure. If my telephone bills this year are anything to
go by, British Telecom have already made a mint out of this one!

The phone lines between Manchester and Blackpool buzzed incessantly over the seven months of intense work that went into chronicling
the career of one of the most powerful and recognisable figures in British
sport. Preparing the manuscript entailed perhaps 60 hours of taped
conversations between Wade and myself, not to mention half-a-dozen
face-to-face sessions at Preston Grasshoppers – or perhaps face to chest
would be more accurate! Then there was the constant liaison over
revision and final detail. Having said that, those who know me insist the
entire operation could have been completed in half the time but for the
fact that I could talk the hind-leg off a proverbial donkey (no rugby
connotation Wade, I insist!).

Without the support and tacit approval of our respective wives, Lynn
and Sharon, the project would never have got off the ground. This year
Wade spent his first summer at home since 1986, yet I suspect Sharon
saw little more of him than had he been touring with England or the
British Lions. As for poor Lynn, saddled with a partner who was
invariably rattling the keys of his word-processor until 3 a.m. or later,
she insists she has forgotten what it's like to have a husband. To both of
them, thanks for all your encouragement and help.

The support and advice of a number of other people has also been
invaluable, first and foremost Bill Campbell, Peter MacKenzie and their
ever-so-helpful staff at Mainstream, without whose backing this book
may never have been published. I would also like to mention particularly
my friends and colleagues in journalism, Gordon Watts and Mark Harris,
who have injected ideas and helpful observations throughout the compilation of the book.

Finally, the kind donation of photographs by some of the best rugby snappers in the business has proved a godsend in helping to make the project viable. So our heartfelt thanks to Tom Jenkins, Colin Elsey, Russell Cheyne and the various newspapers and agencies who allowed us to use their pictures free of charge particularly the *Daily Telegraph*, *Allsport* and *Colorsport*.

GERRY GREENBERG, July 1992

Foreword

by Bill Beaumont
ENGLAND'S 1980 GRAND SLAM CAPTAIN

WHILE I am both delighted and flattered to be asked to write this Foreword, it is one of my greatest regrets in rugby that I never had the opportunity to play with my Lancashire compatriot Wade Dooley. I didn't play *against* him either, but I would definitely have preferred to be on the same side . . . particularly with a four-and-a-half inch height disadvantage!

Although I had retired by the time Wade arrived on the international scene, our respective careers followed a remarkable parallel. We come from the same area, played in the same position for England (although I was a front-of-the-lineout jumper), and went on to make a record number of appearances for our country as lock forwards.

That it was Wade who finally toppled my 34-cap record was particularly apt. I knew it would eventually be beaten and what better than for it to fall to another Lancashire lad, and one I get on well with at that!

My earliest memories of Wade are of a training session at Fylde one evening in the late '70s. Suddenly it went dark as this enormous figure ran around the ground. In those days, it was extremely rare to see a man of his size and the reaction was predictable. 'Who the hell is that?' people would ask. Wade had come down to Fylde with a couple of his police pals but at that time he didn't take his rugby seriously and just drifted away.

Later, he reappeared at Preston and I was fortunate enough to watch his development into a top-class international forward. Even in those early days I could see he possessed a lot of unharnessed talent to go with his giant physique. A good big 'un is always better than a good little 'un, and he also had a fine mentor at Grasshoppers in England's then coach Dick Greenwood.

But for Dick's influence, Wade may well have languished in junior rugby for much longer. However, the secret of success is to make the most of your breaks – which is precisely what he did in becoming the first England lock to amass 50 caps. He showed great single-mindedness and developed a unique ability to lift himself successfully from moderate club level to the summit of English rugby. Nobody else has managed to bridge such a wide chasm, and no one else ever will.

Wade's other unusual gift is that he is able to train and motivate himself alone. I would have found that sort of routine extremely difficult since, like most other players, I needed to train in a group environment to produce the best results.

In latter years, Wade and Paul Ackford linked up to form an outstanding combination in the England second row. By Wade's own admission, Paul's arrival took a hell of a lot of pressure off him and their dual contribution helped to turn England into the enviable force they are in world rugby today.

If he has one regret, I suspect if may be that he never toured New Zealand or South Africa with the British Lions. That he missed out was due to circumstances and politics, though he was, of course, a key member of the successful Lions team that won in Australia in 1989. Yet had he played in my day I am sure he would have completed the 'full set'.

Wade can justifiably feel proud of his achievements on the rugby field. After scaling the dizzy heights of two Grand Slams and a World Cup final, he can look back with pride both on his own performances and the team displays which have put England head and shoulders above any other Five Nations country.

Elsewhere in this book, Wade refers to a scenario of sitting in front of the TV in short pants watching me play for England. Bearing in mind that I retired at 29, all I can say is that he must have been a pretty big lad in short pants!

Happy retirement, Wade . . . if and when you decide to go. It's been a privilege to know you and I hope we'll continue to be friends for years to come.

BILL BEAUMONT, June 1992.

CHAPTER ONE

The Golden Boy

IT ended as it began; like a fairytale. There I was, seven years and 50 caps after being plucked from obscurity, leading England into battle on the day Rugby Union history was created at Twickenham. And I will never forget that golden moment when 60,000 fans erupted as the boys followed me out for the match against Wales that brought us our second successive Grand Slam.

It was the culmination of my eighth and final season as an England player, and I had made a conscious decision at the start of the campaign that I was going to savour this one more than any other. As I was planning for it to be my farewell year, I wanted to take in absolutely everything; to enjoy every last moment of the build-up as if each game was my last.

In preparing for the Wales game I had adopted an approach I had meticulously avoided before and concentrated on keeping free of injury. It's a counter-productive measure because if you give anything less than 100 per cent in club games it's a fair bet you *will* get hurt. However, this was one match I simply had to play in. Apart from its tremendous significance in establishing a second successive Grand Slam for England, it really *was* to be my final fling and I desperately wanted to reach that magical figure of 50 caps.

I had been hoping, almost praying in fact, that skipper Will Carling would let me lead the side out, just as Rory Underwood and Peter Winterbottom had done on their 50th appearances. For me this was the ultimate occasion, the perfect moment to call it a day and go out on an unparalleled high. However, there was no way I could put pressure on Will by *asking* for the privilege of taking over his duties for those few fleeting seconds. That would merely have put pressure on him and been totally unfair. After all, the poor guy had hardly done the job all season!

What I would have done had I not been given the honour, I have no idea. Laughingly, I envisaged a scenario with me sidling up behind Will in the tunnel as we waited to take the field, handing him off, snatching the ball and racing out on to the pitch! I need not have worried. The skipper pulled me aside in training on the Friday and told me the job was mine if I wanted it. His generosity was a measure of the man. He didn't need to ask a second time, either – I nearly bit his hand off. That was it, the icing on the proverbial cake. The only ingredients missing now were a victory and the unlikeliest bonus of all; crowning my golden day by scoring a try.

Winters and I joked about the try situation in the team coach on the way to the game. Peter is a quiet guy and it takes time to get to know him, but during the months since the 1991 World Cup he and I had become closer than ever. He had always been a couple of caps ahead of me and I seemed to have been playing catch-up throughout my England career.

I had given up hope of overtaking him in the cap stakes but even now there was one area I could still steal a march on him, and that was in try-scoring. We were locked together, neck and neck after half-a-century of games . . . with two apiece! 'I'll score today and make it 3–2,' I assured Winters, not believing for one moment it would really happen.

We started off sensationally with a first-minute Carling try, and when we led 15–0 after 28 minutes it looked as if it would be a 40 or 50-point job. But all credit to the Welsh, they stuck to their policy of defending and spoiling and they did it very well. The upshot was a 30-minute period in the second half which was pretty chronic as we pressurised them and they defended like demons. Then Rob Andrew made a break into the Welsh 22 and looked for support. Nine times out of ten he would have slipped the ball the other way; this time, for some reason, he popped it inside to me. I was about ten yards out (though at the time I'd have sworn it was at least 15!) with Welsh scrum-half Robert Jones blocking my way to the line.

The noise from the stands was deafening, while on the pitch players were shouting all around me. As I took the ball my eyes homed in on the try-line; it was like a red rag to a bull. I put absolutely everything into one final surge, focusing my sights on Jones. There were no thoughts of trying to sidestep. I just ploughed straight at him, determined to go right through him if necessary for the four points that meant so much to me. I thought, 'If I get past Jones, I'm there.' A moment later little Robert disappeared under my feet, Micky Skinner and Dean Richards gave me an extra shove from behind – and referee Ray Megson raised his arm to signal a try.

I had done it; I'd scored only the third try of my England career – on my farewell appearance! Where Winters was at that moment I have no idea, but he insisted afterwards that he was right in there pulling me back! I threw the ball up in delight as I rose to my knees, my fists clenched in elation. The din was incredible. Then I looked up at the North Stand, knowing my wife Sharon was up there somewhere. It was a sea of celebration; every last man and woman seemed to be on their feet sharing my golden moment.

There was no chance of seeing Sharon, of course. In any case I discovered later that she had been sitting inside an RFU hospitality box watching it all on television. However, the way things turned out I was pleased she decided to make the trek to London. Since she was expecting our second child just days after the game, I had suggested it might be wise to give this one a miss. But she was adamant she wanted to be there for my final game and, basically, she overruled me. 'It's your last game so I'm going,' she insisted, and that was that. In the event, one of my police colleagues, John Whitaker, drove her down from Blackpool and she spent Friday night as a guest of Paul and Susie Ackford.

Sharon apart, I was certainly not lacking in personal support. My parents were there, as ever, courtesy of the Hoppers boys who picked them up in Warrington on their way down to London. Then there were my colleagues from the Blackpool police, who never missed a game and always congregated in the same place, close to the players' tunnel. The contingent on this occasion numbered around twenty and, as usual, there was no need for me to go looking for them. We had our usual pre-match chat before I got changed, and there was nothing different about the rest of my pre-match routine, either – with one small exception.

Just before taking the field, I always followed the same sentimental ritual of removing my wedding ring and placing it with the photographs I kept in my jacket of Sharon and our daughter Sophie. However, as the big moment approached, my mind became so preoccupied with leading the side out – and all the ribbing the boys had given me over it – that for the first time in my international career I completely forgot to take off the ring.

No one noticed the lapse until the game had been going for a good ten minutes. We were reforming a scrum which for some reason had broken up, and as I grabbed hold of Jeff Probyn, Welsh hooker Garin Jenkins spotted the gold ring gleaming on my finger and immediately informed referee Megson. It had to come off, of course, since it was not taped up and was potentially dangerous. I wanted our physio, Kevin Murphy, to be called on to take it into safe keeping, but Mr Megson insisted on lobbing it towards the touchline . . . straight into the long grass. I had visions of myself scrambling around the pitch after the game looking for it, and perhaps never seeing it again. But fortunately one of the young ball boys realised my dilemma and as play continued, he rooted around in the turf where the ring had landed and recovered it.

If that was a stroke of good fortune, it was truly miraculous how I managed to leave the pitch at the end with the one souvenir I wanted more than anything – the match ball. Sharon and I have jokingly put it down to the fact that she spent the game in the company of that amazing man Terry Waite. It certainly seemed that someone was looking down kindly on me from above!

It was only after the game that I learnt the Archbishop of Canterbury's special envoy was seated alongside Sharon, and when he discovered who she was, he more or less adopted me as if I were his own son! After I scored my try they were apparently dancing around together in celebration; so perhaps it *was* divine providence that completed my day so perfectly. The occasion meant so much to me personally that I desperately wanted to take the ball back to Hoppers. However, knowing the Twickenham fans, it was a remote possibility at best. If past experience was anything to go by, the ball would be the first thing to disappear into the hands of the souvenir hunters. Nothing is sacred from them, as Will Carling discovered after the 1991 Grand Slam when they pinched his boots as they carried him off the field!

The moment of truth came just after Jon Webb's penalty had rounded off the scoring at 24–0. I was running back towards the centre spot when Mr Megson blew for the final time. I looked around to see where the ball was . . . and it came bobbling along virtually to my feet! I couldn't believe my luck, but there was no way anyone was going to get it off me. I picked it up, tucked it under my jersey for safety and made a swift charge for the tunnel. The idea was to get off the pitch as quickly as possible. In the massive celebrations that followed, no one was safe. Even Micky Skinner admitted later that the crush had scared him, while Brian Moore also found it nerve-wracking – and he was on somebody's shoulders!

The reception the Twickenham crowd reserved for me when I led the side out, and again when I scored, was something special; so was the reaction of my team-mates. They knew just how much the occasion meant to me, and their back-slaps and congratulations told me they were as delighted for me as I was myself. With the possible exception of winning the World Cup, nothing could have topped that final day full of excitement, achievement, pride and emotion. It was everything I dreamed it would be – and more.

In fact, I suddenly found myself tugging with my own conscience. I was 34, fitter than I had ever been, so could I *really* leave all this behind – the excitement, the glamour, my army of England mates? There was also the mouth-watering prospect of a first-ever game against South Africa coming up in the autumn, the one major rugby nation I had never played against. My mind had been made up. I was quitting international rugby. But maybe, just maybe, after a quiet and restful summer at home with my family . . . who could predict how I would feel?

I made sure all the boys autographed the ball and tucked it away in my bag, a memento that would in time take pride of place in the display cabinet back at Hoppers.

The celebrating began straight after the match. Bottles of champagne were thrust into our hands and the bubbly flowed freely as Will led us up on to the West Stand balcony to acknowledge the fans' cheers and join in an impromptu singalong.

Back in the changing-room, Skins reserved his own special tribute for me. I'd had my shower, shaved, and was sitting there taking the tape off my ankles when . . . whoosh! Suddenly I was swimming in ice-cold Gatorade, the all-in-one drink the players use for extra energy. If England's No. 1 practical joker wasn't gateauing somebody he was bucketing them; in my case the weapon was the big orange tub full of sticky Gatorade and ice cubes.

Micky's little show of affection sent me scurrying back to the shower, which delayed my planned appearance at the post-match Press conference with Will and team manager Geoff Cooke. When I finally reached the Rose Room to see Sharon and my folks, the first person I met was Terry Waite.

He was a big man in every way, almost as big as me physically, with a bubbling personality to match. His outgoing character completely masked the horror of his five years as a hostage in Lebanon; a nightmare that had ended just a few months earlier. Surely someone who had suffered such a trauma would be more introverted, I thought. Yet here was a man who would be the life and soul of any party. Sharon had taken to him immediately and I could see why. There was an aura about the guy; something intangible that told you he was special. His remarkable sense of humour shone through when Sharon asked him if he was a rugby fan. 'Yes,' he replied, 'but I've not been able to take in too many games of late.'

Skipper Carling paid his own tribute to the troops at the after-match dinner, and gave a mention in dispatches to yours truly for my 50 caps and of course the try. As the evening wore on, you would be amazed how spectacular that try became. A couple of sidesteps, two or three dummies – by the end of the night I think I had collected Rob's pass somewhere around the half-way line! It certainly had more significance than my two previous England tries because it was the only one I ever scored at Twickenham. The other came against France in 1986, when I followed the ball over the line in Paris after Jean Condom had tapped it back, and against the USA in the 1987 World Cup.

Now it was all over. The side that had virtually conquered the world over four glorious seasons seemed to be on the verge of breaking up. For all the banter, we had been like one big family and this was the moment of truth. Leaving my friends would be the hardest part of all, but it couldn't go on for ever. Times change, and my life was about to enter a new era. Or so I thought.

It was originally my intention to retire after the 1991 World Cup. Quite a few of my England team-mates, including Ackford, Winters and Probyn, had also decided that if we beat Australia in the final we would call it a day there and then at the beginning of November. I know it would have seemed strange to quit in the middle of the season, but we had spent 18 months building up to what was to be the pinnacle of our careers; and as we were all well the other side of 30 and had won the Grand Slam a few months earlier, there seemed nothing more to achieve in the game.

However, once the disappointment of our World Cup final defeat had faded, I started thinking about the prospect of two successive Grand Slams – and becoming part of the first team to achieve the feat since 1924. Ackers said he couldn't go on; he couldn't motivate himself to train and prepare for the on-coming Five Nations Championship. But for me there was that other incentive of 50 caps. I've never been one for counting my England appearances, other people have done it for me. However, when someone mentioned that the final game of the season against Wales would coincide with my half-century, the temptation was too much. I decided to give the Five Nations one final crack.

The challenge of achieving back-to-back Slams was made all the more difficult because the two most difficult games were away from home. It involved repeating our World Cup victories in Paris and Edinburgh, against opponents who would be that much more determined because of the earlier reverses.

We also went into the tournament with a new coach. After three remarkably successful seasons, Roger Uttley felt he had gone as far as he could and went back to concentrate on his teaching duties at Harrow School. The decision was particularly poignant for me, since Roger's influence had meant a great deal in my early development as an England player. Even during Dick Greenwood's reign, he would take training sessions and spend time working with me on my lineout skills. I was still very raw in the laws of the international jungle, and the advice of a man who had played 23 times for England proved invaluable. It was under Roger that I learned the technique of spreading myself at the lineout, as well as valuable secrets in dealing with the threat of my opposite number.

Uttley's driving influence as forwards coach also had a major bearing on the British Lions' success in Australia in 1989, but the basic problem after the World Cup was that he and England had outgrown each other. For three years Roger had run the show with outstanding success, but he had reached a point where all his knowledge had been imparted and he had nothing more to give. He was only too aware of that fact himself, and his decision to go was by mutual agreement. Now we needed something different; someone fresh with new ideas. We got it with Dick Best, the man who had moulded London into the best divisional side in the country.

Dick was already familiar with the England set-up, having accompanied us on our pre-World Cup tour to Australia and Fiji. His brief was wider than that of his predecessor, whose influence had been largely forward-orientated. Under Roger, the backs had become used to working under Geoff Cooke and calling on the great tactical experience of Rob Andrew. Dick immediately took control of tactics for the whole team, and while Geoff continued to inject ideas, he was now able to stand back more and oversee the operation.

We had just two weeks' build-up to the opening game in Scotland, and in retrospect were perhaps a little complacent about the game – not to mention rusty after our post-World Cup break. The Scots appeared to be in disarray following the retirement of Finlay Calder and John Jeffrey, and just a week before the game they suffered another major blow when scrum-half Gary Armstrong was crocked playing for his club. So maybe there was just a semblance of over-confidence in the back of our minds when we trooped out at Murrayfield for the second time in three months.

The first 40 minutes of that Calcutta Cup game came as a rude awakening. From the start we were slow to the breakdown and struggled for possession; and as a lineout pairing Martin Bayfield and I won very little ball against a Scots side still seething over our World Cup semi-final win.

By half-time I was beginning to wonder if I'd keep my place long enough to reach 50 caps! That the Scots were leading was bad enough; but they had also shunted us over our own line for a pushover try. It was the only time England suffered that ultimate embarrassment during my career, and was all the more difficult to accept because scrummaging had always been one of our greatest strengths.

It came just before the change-round when Scotland were awarded a five-metre scrum. Since Brian Moore had just received attention for a knock on the head, there was probably a lack of concentration on our part as we packed down. However, the Scots surprised us by getting their shove on early, and it certainly didn't help when our back row broke off, leaving five of us to push against eight. There are no gripes about them pushing before the ball came in; at top level you get away with what you can and with our experience we should have known all the tricks. To coin one of Roger Uttley's favourite phrases, it was simply that we were 'a bit dull'.

If any one moment shook us out of our lethargy, that was it. After a commendable first-half performance the new cap Tim Rodber went off with a neck injury to be replaced by Dean Richards – and we immediately tightened things up. Deano, colossus of a player that he is, obviously realised from the sideline what needed to be done, and we did it. Everything revolved around him as we began to drive it through the forwards a lot more, and in the last 20 minutes we took complete control. So much so that we came off the park with a 25–9 victory, England's biggest-ever win on Scottish soil.

Despite our success, the occasion was to be soured for me by subsequent over-reaction to a difference I had with my opposite number, Doddie Weir, in the first half. I had played against the gangling Melrose youngster in the World Cup, and in the intervening period he seemed to have put on some much-needed bulk and was beginning to get to grips with the requirements of top-level rugby. He was also quoted in the newspapers as saying he had been overawed in the World Cup but that was not going to happen again. This time he planned to get stuck into me; and, all credit to him, he did.

In international rugby, you don't just lie down and let your opposite number walk all over you. You have a go at him and try to psyche him out in any way you can. Doddie came out and did just that – and I have the utmost respect for him for doing so. He had a lot to make up for and from the kick-off I felt the weight of a succession of knees and elbows. A sequence of minor incidents followed as our personal battle hotted up. Then, from a drop-out, Doddie whacked me with his elbow on the side of my chin.

The sequel followed moments later when their stand-off, Craig Chalmers, dropped out short, Neil Edwards gathered, and as I ran in to tackle Edwards, Weir was standing in the way. As I went past I caught him on the back of the ear with my elbow. It was not a premeditated attack, purely a spur-of-the-moment reaction, and really just the next instalment in our ongoing battle.

Although Weir was laid out and had to receive attention, referee Derek Bevan did not see exactly what happened, neither did his touch judges. I did not regard it as a sending-off offence, anyway, but I knew I had overstepped the mark by allowing a personal battle to get in the way of my game. Doddie had been intent on winding me up, and he had succeeded – unlike the French intimidation that had been resisted so effectively in the World Cup quarter-final in Paris. Now, by reacting as I did, I had shown the sort of indiscipline England were trying to eradicate.

Weir played on, seemingly with no ill-effects, yet it was claimed later that the blow had perforated his eardrum. All I know is that we had a beer, a chat and a laugh together at the dinner that evening and he seemed none the worse for wear. There were no hard feelings on either side and, as far as we were both concerned, that was the end of the matter.

What happened was nothing new in international rugby. I've been clattered many a time myself; in fact, back in 1986 John Beattie hit me with his elbow in very similar fashion at Murrayfield. He cracked me on the side of the face and my eye closed up, but I didn't go around making a big thing about it. And to Doddie's credit, neither did he.

A week later, when England announced an unchanged team to face Ireland, I suddenly began reading inferences that my international career was on the line as a result of the Weir incident. On the same day as the Calcutta Cup match, there had been another incident in which Welsh lock Tony Copsey had clattered Ireland's Neil Francis, so discipline was very much to the fore at the time. When Geoff Cooke spoke to journalists at the Press conference in which the team to face Ireland was announced, they got the inference that I had been pulled to one side and told in no uncertain terms that any further lapse would mean I would never reach my 50th cap. That was simply not the case; there had been no such lecture. All that happened was that at our weekend team meeting, Geoff stood up and talked to us generally about our indiscipline and complacency against the Scots.

John Jeffrey – a former British Lions colleague, no less – suggested on a television chat show in Scotland that my offence was so heinous I should be banned from rugby for life. His playing career just over, he was obviously trying to make a name for himself as a media man, and his statement was splashed across two pages in one of the tabloid dailies. Coming from JJ it was quite something because, having been on tour with him, I was well aware that the Shark also had skeletons in his cupboard.

What angered not only myself, but many of my England teammates, was that he had himself suddenly become whiter than white and fully qualified to pontificate on the behaviour of others. It was only a couple of months earlier that Jeffrey's bosom buddy Finlay Calder had blatantly taken out Irish fullback Jim Staples in similar circumstances in the World Cup. OK, he got away with it, but I don't remember JJ crying condemnation with the rest of us over that incident.

It was also significant that none of the Scots side who faced us that day, including Doddie Weir and coach Ian McGeechan, made any adverse comment about the incident. In fact, McGeechan actually made light of the whole thing when he was asked after the game about the significance of Weir's perforated eardrum. I'm told he replied: 'It means we can see straight through him.'

The home game against Ireland may have looked a formality to some people, but there was certainly no complacency on the part of the England players. After our performance against the Scots we were, if anything, a little concerned as to the outcome. After all, it was only a short time since the Irish had come within a whisker of knocking the Aussies out of the World Cup. In the event we scored a try in the first couple of minutes and it was probably the worst thing that could have happened! For some reason we sat back on our laurels and as the Irish pummelled away at us, the inevitable happened. A Ralph Keyes try put them right back in it and, their confidence soaring, they forced us to soak up more and more pressure. Yet not for one moment did I seriously think we would lose. Such was the confidence in the side that defeat was something we never contemplated in any game. Just as we had done at Murrayfield, we dug deep, stepped up our game . . . and coasted to a 38–9 victory. It was our best-ever result against the Irish and our second record score of the season.

Then it was on to Paris for our second tangle with the French at Parc des Princes in four months. The World Cup quarter-final had been unusual in that we changed our base, but now we went back to all-too-familiar surroundings at the Trianon Palace Hotel in Versailles.

We had always stayed there since my first trip to France in 1986, when I scored my first try for England and then found myself witness to some costly late-night revelry. It was the only time I can remember an England team getting out of hand and really it was the fault of the respective committees for not providing any form of entertainment at the hotel.

The high jinks started after most of us had been bussed back to the Trianon following the post-match dinner in Paris, only to find the place dead. It was scarcely midnight, and there we were in sleepy Versailles after our final game of the season with nothing to do but provide our own action. So, pepped up by a few more beers, courtesy of the Nike representative, the boys decided to liven up the proceedings as only rugby players can. Fortunately we were up on the top floor, away from all the other guests, because it was some party as a dozen players turned fire extinguishers on each other, tipped up plant pots and kicked in locked doors. Brian Ashton, our assistant coach, didn't know what hit him as Richard Hill and Gareth Chilcott stormed into his room, extinguishers gushing foam, and saturated everything from the ceiling and walls to his open suitcase and neatly hung-up blazer and trousers.

Since we were leaving early on the Sunday, Brian had done most of his packing and was already in bed. He was not amused at having to travel home in jeans, and Hill and Chilcott were later hit by a £300 bill from the hotel for the damage the impromptu 'party' had caused. It wasn't that they were the only guilty ones, just that they weren't as streetwise as the rest, who made themselves scarce once Brian's room went in.

Anyway, that sort of behaviour was the last thing on anyone's mind as we checked into the Trianon before the 1992 French game. Swayed no doubt by the brutality of the World Cup quarter-final, the Press proceeded to build it into another potential war. In reality, it was nothing like as bad – although in the closing minutes the frustrated French managed to lose their heads again to the point that two of their forwards were sent off. Coach Pierre Berbizier's logic in selecting the team seemed strange, to say the least. On the one hand he preached to the world about the need for more discipline, then he seemed to go totally against that principle by picking a nucleus of the notorious 'Beasts of Begles' pack.

On top of that, I simply could not understand Berbizier's reasoning in playing Begles lock Christophe Mougeot in preference to Olivier Roumat, the man I rated France's best lock. It certainly made my job a lot easier as we went for a third successive win at Parc des Princes. For the third time in as many games, we had to soak up a considerable amount of first-half pressure. But while the French pack produced some inspired driving rugby, our defence lived up to the great reputation for solidity it had built over the previous couple of seasons. Then, calmly, we stepped up our usual couple of gears . . . and as the game slipped away from them the French forwards exploded in a powder-keg of indiscipline.

Gregoire Lascube, an Agen CID officer no less, had been putting himself around a fair bit, as he had done against us in the World Cup. On that occasion he cracked me in the ear and deafened me. This time he came flying through a ruck to clatter me again – and once again I ignored his excesses. But when he stamped on Martin Bayfield, then callously looked behind to see what damage he'd done and promptly repeated the act, referee Stephen Hilditch had no option but to send him packing. Lascube had broken one of the game's unwritten laws; he had deliberately aimed his boot at a rival forward's head. Okay, players who lie over the ball expect to get raked and rucked legally; that is all part and parcel of the game. But the accepted rule among players is that you *never* go anywhere near an opponent's head. Lascube's behaviour was unforgivable, and he deserved everything he got – including the six-month ban the French imposed on him immediately afterwards.

Minutes after Lascube's departure, France were down to 13 men after hooker Vincent Moscato, who had switched to prop following the departure of Lascube, went completely berserk right in front of the referee. If frustration at the scoreline and the added insult of having his prop sent off were not enough, poor Moscato was being turned inside out by Jeff Probyn in his role as emergency loose-head.

When he tried to head-butt Probes as a scrum went down, Mr Hilditch tapped him on the forehead and made it clear he would be off if it happened again. As the scrum re-formed, Brian Moore passed the word through that he thought things were about to blow up again. Since the hands of our front-row trio were effectively tied, the contingency plan was for the boys behind to break up quickly and jump in to prevent any trouble.

In the event, it was not necessary. Moscato was babbling away in French to acting hooker Jean-Francois Tordo, tears of rage pouring down his cheeks – and as the scrum went down he tried it on with Jeff again. Probes merely took a dive so the intended blow failed to connect; and Moscato joined Lascube for an early bath. The poor guy had flipped completely. In fact, I'm sure I've picked up saner people at work and thrown them into the back of a police van!

The game lost, the French front-row lunacy even got to Philippe Gimbert, another Begles man and lone survivor of the trio who started the game. When Jason Leonard pushed him away, he took a ridiculous dive backwards clutching his head and trying to make out he had been head-butted in the way Probes had. They had gone completely – and now only Wales stood between us and rugby folklore.

Although we started hot favourites, with such high stakes there was never the slightest danger of us underestimating the Welsh, for all their problems. But even the 24–0 victory which completed a new Championship record of 118 points – not to mention that second Grand Slam – could not satisfy the likes of David Campese. In Aussie eyes, it seems we had merely beaten four bad teams.

I totally reject that view; in fact Campo's views, as expressed in a television interview immediately after the tournament, merely denigrate the opposition. I wonder what he expected us to do to prove ourselves? Perhaps he felt we should have been winning by 60 points instead of 25 and 30.

The fact is no side can do more than win all their games – and win them near enough by record margins. I certainly won't knock the Australians, but I'd just like to see whingeing Wallabies like Campese go to both Paris and Murrayfield twice in four months and win all four games as we did on our way to the World Cup final and 1992 Grand Slam.

CHAPTER TWO

Deaf and Glory

THE Parc des Princes has always been a daunting place. But this was brutal – the toughest game of my life.

Inside the concrete cauldron the atmosphere was electric. We had become used to the pre-match hype from previous visits, with the parachutists dropping in, bands blaring on the terraces, tickertape, firecrackers and cockerels chased by harassed officials. You could have been excused for thinking you were at a Latin-American football fiesta rather than the 1991 Rugby World Cup quarter-final.

The build-up had taken its usual Paris course. Police outriders giving our coach the VIP treatment with a motor-cycle escort through the traffic at breakneck speed. Whistles blowing, kicking the sides of stray cars that wouldn't move over, roaring through red lights as if they weren't there. It was difficult for the boys to concentrate on the job in hand, and most players would readily admit that they sat glued to the antics of the motor-cycle police on our journey from Versailles to the stadium. If my colleagues in England behaved like that they would be drummed out of the force. Or even arrested. Was it some obscure French plot to put us off our game, I wondered.

There had been little difference to our normal routine after we reached the ground, even if this *was* the greatest tournament in rugby. As usual, we'd all strolled on to the park to look at the playing surface and soak up the pre-match atmosphere. Then it was into the changing-room . . . and the big build-up to kick-off. My own routine never varied. First I would strip down to my trunks and shorts, then it was in to physio Kevin Murphy to have my ankles strapped and the Deep Heat rubbed in. Next, on with the socks, shinpads and shirt, then the headband and my boots. Finally that sentimental little ritual – removing my wedding ring and placing it with the photos of Sharon and Sophie. Then off to a quiet corner for 20 minutes or so to stretch off and psyche myself up for the battle to come.

Most of the big rugby stadiums have a totally separate shower area, and Paris is no different. I went in and got on with it. On the whole the England dressing-room is a pretty tranquil place, with each player preparing for the game in his own way. Peter Winterbottom, for instance, tended to be quiet like myself. Then you had guys like Brian Moore babbling away incessantly; but no one would rant and rave like some of the Scots did on the 1989 British Lions tour. When they started banging heads, screaming and thumping each other, I just got out of the way. It was difficult enough keeping a straight face, let alone try to psyche myself up like that.

I warmed up, quietly and alone, detached from the rest of the boys and concentrating on the job I had to do on my opposite number. I went through all the calls in my own mind and there were 1,001 things going on in my head as I did my stretches and loosened off, then went back into the changing-room.

Team doctor Ben Gilfeather was doing the rubs while Kevin Murphy was still busy on strappings. As the minutes ticked away, team manager Geoff Cooke and coach Roger Uttley stood quietly, imparting the odd word of encouragement and advice to individual players.

I went through some final lineout details with my second-row partner Paul Ackford. The back-row boys were having a similar discussion among themselves, so were half-backs Rob Andrew and Richard Hill. Gradually the backroom boys and bench reserves began to drift out of the changing-room, leaving just Smurf to do the final preparations. We were on our own with perhaps ten minutes to kick-off. Skipper Will Carling called everyone together, though by now all the talking had been done. There was time for just one final gee-up. We formed a circle, with captain Carling in the middle calling for heroics from his troops. Basically it was do or die, sudden death; we needed no reminding. Players looked anxiously at each other, sweating from the exertions of private and collective warm-ups. The oppressive atmosphere of the claustrophobic changing-room was almost overpowering. A couple of tight squeezes, then it was out into the tunnel, forwards leading the way.

Paris is unique in that the teams come out of opposite changing-rooms then line up a few feet apart, divided by officials, waiting to go out on to the pitch. This time the intensity was greater than ever. The forwards looked across, and picked out their opposite numbers. It was eyeball-to-eyeball time. Not a word spoken – just a silent glare across

the tunnel to try and psyche the other guy out as TV cameras closed in
to catch every facial expression. Then the signal came and out we strode
into the daylight . . . and the cacophony of sound and colour that is
uniquely the Parc des Princes. The battle was about to commence.

Perhaps it is just as well I didn't see the barrage of French fists that
knocked Nigel Heslop senseless in the opening five minutes. Otherwise
it's possible I would have ruined the master plan that won us the game.
The tactic was simple. We were not going to retaliate, however much
they baited us with familiar French tactics like gouging and punching in
the scrums. My idea was just to laugh at them, whatever happened. On
other occasions we'd have responded in a completely different way but
this time the instruction was to step back, whatever the temptation. And
for some of us, particularly battle-hardened forwards like myself, that
isn't always as easy as it sounds. Take the Heslop incident, for example.
I mean, you don't just leave one of your own boys to get a pasting from
three or four unruly Frenchmen.

As it was, I was right up there behind Nigel when he tackled Serge
Blanco as he took that high ball on his own line. But I finished up
charging into French lock Olivier Roumat and barrelling away to the
left, so all I saw at the time was the wall of blue shirts surrounding
Blanco.

Then there was the sickening sight of Nigel sprawled on the
ground, unconscious. I was not to discover precisely how it happened
until I saw the video after the game.

Mike Teague, Jason Leonard and Paul Ackford were quickly in
there to assist Heslop, but their reactions were commendably restrained.
They held back their emotions – and, as the game progressed, proceeded
to turn the other cheek to all the flak the French hurled in our direction.
My left ear took such a dig from prop Gregoire Lascube's fist early on
that I was half-deaf for most of the game and later had to see a specialist.
But we kept our cool under great provocation and the inevitable
happened. The French started bitching and back-biting among themselves, became more and more undisciplined, and the whole pattern of
their game was upset.

The fact I had to keep asking for lineout calls to be repeated because
of partial deafness didn't matter. I never doubted that victory, and a
place in the semi-final, would be ours. Even when France pulled back to
10–10 and English supporters' hearts started fluttering as wildly as those
cockerels that invariably find their way on to the Paris pitch.

If any one moment inspired us it was Micky Skinner's stunning tackle on Marc Cecillon – lifting his opposite number and driving him backwards in one tremendous moment of defiance as France attacked from a five-metre scrum. What a way to relieve the pressure!

Skipper Carling duly confirmed our superiority with a late try, driven over the line by the forwards, to complete a 19–10 victory, our third in a row in Paris. Once the game was over all I wanted to do was celebrate. Returning to the changing-room to find my number had been drawn out of the hat to be drugs tested, I wandered straight along to the medical room through the public area – gloating at any Frenchman who happened to be standing by. They weren't interested in me but there was some frenzied action going on in the approaches to the French changing-room. As I had a urine sample to provide for testing, I didn't take too much notice at the time. But later I learnt of French coach Daniel Dubroca's outrageous behaviour towards referee David Bishop – behaviour that was to cost him his job.

Dubroca subsequently resigned in the aftermath of his physical and verbal aggression towards Mr Bishop, but at least he took the honourable way out. Knowing the former French skipper, his behaviour seemed totally out of character, yet on this occasion he clearly overstepped the mark. I might not be an angel but I have learnt over the years that what the referee says is sacrosanct, both on and off the pitch. As far as I am concerned his word is law.

That victory in Paris was the highlight of a tournament that took us to the brink of the greatest achievement the game has to offer . . . winning the 1991 World Cup. It was a marvellous experience just to be part of the biggest sporting tournament Britain had staged for a quarter of a century – even if from a playing point of view it did start dismally with that depressing 18–12 defeat by New Zealand in the opening game.

The build-up to the World Cup had been phenomenal. The tournament had grabbed the public's interest and the atmosphere as the competition approached was tremendous. We started getting mail by the sackload . . . and while Dame Kiri Te Kanawa was soaring towards No. 1 in the hit parade with *World in Union*, the players even got to No. 16 with our own version of *Swing Low Sweet Chariot*.

The recording was arranged for the first week in August, and we duly arrived at the Abbey Road studios, situated in the suburbs of St Johns Wood, NW8, early on a Sunday morning. After breakfast, we got stuck into the serious business of producing the squad World Cup record, surrounded by Beatles memorabilia. In its entire 60-year history

I don't think the studio had ever heard anything quite like our first rendition. After producing stars like Elton John, the Rolling Stones and The Who, to name but a few, we were awful . . . bad enough to have made poor John Lennon turn in his grave! So bad, indeed, that the producer threw his hands in the air in dismay and was ready to walk out.

However, we did manage to get it right in the end, even if Paul Ackford was under strict instructions to stand at the back and just mime the words for the video. Ackers is so tone deaf it's untrue; the worst I've ever heard. In fact, when he used to stand next to me for the national anthem it took me all my time to keep a straight face. The video also featured me retracing the Beatles' illustrious footsteps, along with Brian Moore, Rob Andrew and Rory Underwood, as we walked across the pedestrian crossing outside the studios immortalised on the famous Abbey Road LP cover.

For all Ackers' harmony problems, some of the players had pretty fair voices. Dewi Morris was one of course – he's a Welshman so it's natural. Brian Moore also fancied himself as a bit of a crooner . . . but he's hardly a glamour boy when it comes to looks. And Rob Andrew was chirping away down in the front row with that boy-soprano voice of his.

It was all great fun . . . but there were more serious things on our minds. Most people don't realise it, but the England players had been preparing for the biggest challenge of our careers for fully 18 months. We all had individual fitness schedules mapped out on wall charts that told us exactly when we should be peaking, when to rest, when to step it up again and what type of training to do at different times of the year. If you couldn't keep to those schedules then you only had yourself to blame. But what an anti-climax that All Blacks disaster turned out to be.

Quite simply, we froze. The champagne occasion went flat in front of a packed Twickenham crowd and millions of TV viewers the world over. The whole occasion overtook the game and we were overawed by their reputation as world champions and the fact it was eight years since they had last visited Twickenham. In short, we just didn't play as we can. We also knew that, barring a sensation, we would still be in the quarter-final. Let's face it, Italy and the USA were never going to beat either ourselves or New Zealand. The only imponderable was which of us would qualify as Pool One winners and which as runners-up. Even before the tournament started we knew we'd be playing France in Paris or the Pool Four runners-up in Lille. And although France would be the tougher test, with our recent impressive record in Paris, it really didn't make that much difference to us.

It was just unfortunate that we didn't give our supporters much to cheer about against the All Blacks, particularly one brave paraplegic fan called Dave Byrne who wheeled himself fully three miles from the Star and Garter Services Hospital at the top of Richmond Hill to watch the game. He went missing in his wheelchair before the match and apparently bumped himself up and down pavements and roads all the way to Twickenham, where he bluffed his way in by talking to one of the policemen, who pushed him up the tunnel from where he watched the game. Ten minutes before the end, disappointed with the way things were going and in order to beat the rush, he turned round and wheeled himself back up to the hospital. Some time later Ackers and I met him when we went up to record an ITV video piece. The journey had taken so much out of him that he was still laid up in bed, exhausted. It brought home to me just how lucky I am to be fit . . . and the remarkable dedication of an England supporter like Dave.

I would probably have played against both Italy and the States but for a freak knee injury that made me a bit of a laughing stock among the rest of the squad. After the All Blacks game, we'd flown up to Leeds to watch Italy beat the States at Otley, then returned to Tinley Hall to prepare for our own game against the Italians.

I had just collected the ball from a training drop-out and was kicking it back to David Pears when my studs caught in the grass and I wrenched my knee. Still, it could have been worse – I'd have had a lot more trouble explaining it had I picked up the injury in one of the impromptu drop-kicking competitions the forwards used to hold while we waited for the backs to join us on the practice pitch. But it still meant that instead of playing I ended up watching from the stands as the boys thumped Italy.

Fortunately I was able to have some pretty intensive physio on the knee over the next couple of days. One of the good things about being locked away with the squad is that you can lie on the physio's couch all day receiving treatment if necessary. I was also able to test it out in the 37–9 win against the USA, a game which, as the score suggests, we coasted through fairly comfortably.

The quarter-final was where the real action started – and I was still feeling the aftermath right up to the final two weeks later. Lascube's punch caused me a few anxious moments, particularly when I started bleeding from inside the ear the following day. It crossed my mind that the deafness which had confused my interpretation of the lineout calls might be a long-term thing, but when Ben Gilfeather examined me he insisted my hearing would return to normal in time. When the problem persisted, I went to see a specialist just before the final and he diagnosed bruising to the inner canal of the ear. Sure enough, the deafness finally wore off – and that was quite a relief.

Seven days after Paris came an equally daunting challenge . . . to beat the Scots at Murrayfield. We had failed to do it in the Grand Slam showdown some 20 months earlier, when we started firm favourites. And although this game was if anything even more important, somehow the build-up and atmosphere in the hotbed of Scottish rugby was not quite so intimidating.

In fact, the week was filled with light-hearted banter between ourselves and the Scottish fans. No sooner had we returned from Paris than we were flying up to Edinburgh for the semi-final – and our base slap-bang in the centre of the Scottish capital at the Carlton Highland Hotel.

Normally we would stay out at Peebles, well away from the city and the fans, although from my own point of view staying in town presents no problems whatsoever. I love the banter, it's something I get a lot of in my job as a policeman in Blackpool. And despite the importance of the game there was not a hint of intimidation or nastiness in the build-up to the semi-final.

We were all able to go to a couple of local pubs for a few pints early in the week in the friendliest of surroundings. And when Ackers and I went out for a stroll along Princes Street the night before the game, the atmosphere was buzzing. It was quite late and the Friday night revellers were all out as we walked along the Royal Mile, Paul in his tatty old track-suit and me in my England jacket. One of the most important games of our careers might have been only hours ahead, yet everything was remarkably relaxed.

It was such a good feeling that we both wondered why England had always elected to stay 45 minutes out of Edinburgh in recent years. Obviously others felt the same as we did, because when we returned for the 1992 Five Nations game three months later we found ourselves once again based right in the heart of the city at the Balmoral Hotel.

The atmosphere at the semi-final lacked the intensity of a normal Championship game, presumably because the crowd was not as predominantly Scottish as usual. In fact, with people of so many different nationalities attending the World Cup games, the feeling right through the tournament was not quite the same as in the Five Nations. As it turned out, perhaps Scotland suffered more from the reduced passion than we did.

I won't say it was a case of being bent on revenge for that agonising Grand Slam defeat on our previous visit to Murrayfield, but we were certainly keen to do well. In the event, the game did not go to plan – but the result did. We managed to keep it tight and, eventually, squeeze the Scots out of the game and come away with a narrow 9–6 victory. Our tactics didn't please everyone, however, and we were criticised for not playing a flowing game either at Murrayfield or the previous week in Paris. Nevertheless, that's what we felt we had to do to get the victories we wanted and, as it turned out, on both occasions our game plan was justified by the result. Having said that, the Scots tackling was ferocious, just as it had been in 1990. And when you come up against a defence as tenacious and committed as that, there are only so many ways through.

It was quite a bonus for us when Gavin Hastings fluffed that penalty in front of the posts with the score at 6–6. I had already turned away, having accepted in my own mind that we were about to go 9–6 behind. While the miss amazed me, I couldn't help feeling for a man who had served Scotland so well with his usually reliable boot in recent years. Yet I would not have been over-concerned had the kick gone over because I was convinced we could step up the pace and win the game. One of the spin-offs of the confidence that has been bred into the England side in recent years is that on taking the field we always believe we will win, no matter the opposition.

The icing on the cake came in the dressing-room after the game – and TV commentator Jim Rosenthal felt the full force of it. Jim, who had spent the entire tournament with us as part of ITV's World Cup coverage, was there as usual with his camera crew as we celebrated reaching the final. But the last thing we wanted after our exertions was the tray of sandwiches and large chocolate gateau that had been brought in for us. All the weary players wanted to do was crash out in the bath and then unwind with a beer or a soft drink.

Jim, together with his cameramen and sound recordist, had more or less become part of the squad. Anyway, there he was trying to conduct interviews when John Olver found a more tasty place for the gateau . . . slap in the middle of poor Jim's face. And as if that wasn't embarrassing enough for him, the whole scenario was recorded for posterity on the England World Cup video!

The build-up to the final against Australia was quite something –

with David Campese trying to wind us up and getting on his high horse about our 'boring' play. But anyone who thinks his comments influenced our thinking is dreaming. We were all experienced enough to realise it was just media hype and we promptly put it to the back of our minds and got on with the job in hand.

The fact is we had already decided to change our tactics for the final and open the play more than we had in the earlier games. But to be honest we didn't plan to open up quite as much as we did! We knew we could play that type of rugby extremely effectively. It wasn't foreign to us, as some people tried to make out. In fact, we had done it successfully in the 1990 Five Nations and we were to do it again in 1992.

No successful team plays a carefree, expansive game all the time. The whole idea is to tailor your tactics towards the opposition, which is precisely what we did – and very successfully. Up until the final, that is. And whatever the cynics say, had we not kept it tight against Scotland I reckon we wouldn't have made the final.

We certainly did not lose against Australia because of being unable to adapt. The way the game went we won ample ball and created enough scoring opportunities to have won the Webb Ellis Trophy. It's just that our backs could not make any real headway and the last-ditch tackling of the Wallabies was superb. Two or three men were never really committed to the ruck or maul situation, which gave them cover out wide, whatever we tried. It seemed that any time the ball was spun along the backs, the final pass simply would not go to hand. The blanket Aussie defence would stifle the attack – or the ball would bounce off Rory Underwood's head!

I don't believe for one minute that had we kept it tight the Queen would have ended up presenting the trophy to Will Carling rather than Nick Farr-Jones. The fact is we could never suck enough of the Australians in to break them down. There always seemed to be men over and they had really worked out their defensive tactics very well.

Yet despite their 12–6 victory, I don't think they were a better side than us. In an after-match interview I came out and said that the better side had won. Maybe I should have qualified that by saying the Aussies were the better team overall, taking into account their performances throughout the competition. However, on the day, the side criticised for its negative style won the hearts and minds of everybody watching – we just didn't win the game.

I'd say England certainly had the personnel to beat them. It was just unfortunate that in the final itself things didn't work out for us. We proved up front that we had the artillery to see them off; and as far as the backs are concerned, we did precisely what we needed to do – try to stretch the Aussies by spinning the ball wide. It's just that the last-ditch effort foiled us every time; the final tackle, spilled ball or whatever. The saddest thing for me is that there will never be another chance to make up for it.

CHAPTER THREE

Aiming High

THE midwife at Warrington General Hospital was so impressed with my credentials the day I came into the world that she insisted on parading me around the ward to show the disbelieving maternity patients and staff.

I weighed in at 10lb 10oz, quite a specimen of babyhood in those days. Five years later my brother Paul was to beat me heads down when he made his grand entrance at exactly 11 pounds. However, on 2 October 1957, Wade Anthony Dooley was up there on his own; and from that day onwards I have always been on the large side.

My parents Geoff and Ethel decided to call me Wade after hearing the name from friends at the United States air base at nearby Burton-wood. The military police used to mix a lot with the local police and their families and apparently the name just cropped up in conversation. My wife has done a bit of research and discovered that it is actually an old Anglo-Saxon name, though hardly common in this country. In fact, I have only come across it perhaps half-a-dozen times, including one flattering occasion at an England training session not so long ago. A man came up and asked for my autograph, explaining: 'It's for my son. Please make it out to Wade – we named him after you.'

My father and mother, who in those days was Ethel Wright, met when they were working at Crossfields soap and chemical company, now Lever Brothers, and to this day one of the biggest employers in Warrington. Dad's family were from the Cheshire village of Stretton, some ten miles from Warrington, where my grandfather William Dooley was a farm labourer. Old Bill's greatest passion was working with the farm's Shire horses and taking them to all the local shows. While Dad and his sister Barbara had a rural upbringing, Bill and my grandmother, Winifred, eventually moved to Warrington, where he later became a fireman at Crossfields.

My great-aunt Margaret, who is now in her mid-nineties, has always been the family oracle and has traced the Dooley roots back to Ireland, though long before my time. She is convinced the family is descended from a Dublin barrister who came to live in England and later moved on to the United States.

Dad, who is himself 6ft 5in, joined the police force soon after he met my mother and by the time they got married he was well into his new job. The Dooleys have been steeped in police tradition since the days of my great-grandfather John Winter Turner, Winifred's father, who was a sergeant in Warrington soon after the turn of the century. Later on my great-uncle Tom Dooley became a village bobby in the town while great-aunt Amy was quite a celebrity in Wigan during her time as a WPC. She is a big lady in every way, and was renowned in those days both for her size and the fact she stood for no nonsense. In fact, rumour has it that when Amy was around the local villains used to run for cover. Like most of the Dooleys she is a six-footer and actually built herself a reputation for sorting out pub fights on her own!

With that kind of family background, it was only natural that Dad should follow the police tradition – a tradition that was later to rub off on Paul and myself. As Mum was very much a local girl, it was also natural that my parents' wedding should take place at Christ Church in Warrington, an establishment which was later to play an important part in my own spiritual development. I was christened and confirmed there, attended Rev Caldwell's Sunday school and also spent time as both an altar boy and choirboy. It was quite an accomplished choir, with a large number of local boys enlisted to the fold – and of such a standard that we regularly visited Chester Cathedral for the annual choir festival. Choirboys we may have been, but angels definitely not. We were an unruly bunch, with the vicar and choirmaster both having their work cut out to keep us in check. Many a cassock and surplice would get torn playing British Bulldog on the lawns of the church prior to a wedding . . . later requiring invisible mending at mother's own expense. There was also the occasional internal inquiry into the dropping level of the altar wine bottle.

Needless to say, the highlight for all the boys were the 2/6d Saturday weddings. With Rev Caldwell and the Christ Church conveyor belt working at full speed, two or three weddings during an afternoon and you were talking serious pounds, shillings and pence!

My parents had been married for just a few months when they moved into a brand new police house in Frederick Street, Latchford –

the Warrington suburb on the fringe of the Cheshire countryside where my mother was born. That home was their pride and joy and it was there that Paul and I were to grow up. It was one of four police semis in a street of terraced houses; the greenness of the surrounding school playing fields and farmland contrasting with the grim image of a northern industrial town. My parents still live in the same house, only now it is their own home and Dad, who spent the last eight years of his career on the local beat in Latchford, has long since retired from the police.

Although all my childhood recollections are happy ones, when I was five-and-a-half years old there was a major panic in the family when I contracted viral pneumonia. One moment I was a normal healthy child, then suddenly I lost all interest in everything. Because I didn't want to go to school everyone thought I was pulling a fast one; but then my appetite went too, and when my mother found me flaked out in bed one morning, sweating profusely, she realised this was no con. Our family doctor, Dr Hughes, was summoned urgently – and he promptly put me on an intensive course of drug treatment which he supervised with daily visits.

It was the only serious illness I've had, but although my mum remembers it all too vividly, personally I recall nothing of it. My most abiding memories are of the wonderful family holidays we spent in the Welsh countryside and seaside resorts just a short drive from the north-west of England, and on the Isle of Man. Like all brothers, Paul and I used to fight like mad. With the five-year age gap he was always smaller than me, of course, and at a mere 6ft 4in he still hasn't caught up!

However, as we grew up we found a common bond in rugby, and while Paul never made it to international level he developed into a cracking back-row forward, spending time playing for the likes of Orrell and Waterloo. We played a lot together over the years, both for the police and Preston, and at one time Warrington Rugby League club were seriously interested in signing him.

Warrington is a real hotbed of the 13-man code and until I joined the police cadets it had never crossed my mind to play Rugby Union. League strongholds like Widnes, Wigan and St Helens are all within a few miles and that game was always No. 1 with the family. However, when Dad went into the army for his national service he started playing Union and became quite a handy player himself. He was a lock like me and after being demobbed came through trials for St Helens with flying colours and had an opportunity to turn professional. But then the police gave him an ultimatum; it was either Rugby League or the force, he couldn't do both. At that time the money situation in League was nothing like it is today, there was no security whatsoever. One injury and you were out with nothing to support your wife and family on. So Dad, who was also a top-class swimmer and diver, chose the police.

I don't remember seeing him play rugby, but he regularly took me down to watch Warrington's home games. In those days they played on a Saturday and it was nothing unusual for crowds of 30,000 to attend games at Wilderspool. The town still buzzed with tales of local heroes like Albert Pimblett, Albert Johnson, Harold Palin and Harold Bath; but they had all retired by the time I came along. For me the man of the moment was Brian Bevan, the frail, bald-headed Aussie wing who broke try records galore during his unique 18-year career. And, like most of the sports-mad kids in the town, I had dreams of being a Rugby League pro myself when I grew up.

As Warrington is geographically exactly half-way between the soccer hot-beds of Liverpool and Manchester, there was obviously quite a following in school for the north-west's glamour clubs. Indeed, as a teenager I would stand on the Kop with my mates, cheering on Liverpool stars like Kevin Keegan and John Toshack, and marvel at the superb Anfield atmosphere. But since we had no first-class soccer in Warrington itself, and Rugby Union was confined to the local grammar school, Rugby League was always the main sporting topic in the town and at school.

It was my headmaster at Bolton Council Junior School, John Horrocks, who started me playing the game, along with another teacher called Maurice Seddon. By the time I was nine I was good enough to play Rugby League alongside 11-year-olds in the Ashton Trophy junior cup final. All the big school finals took place on the hallowed Wilderspool ground and I believe I am still one of the youngest boys ever to play there. I have also kept my medal – the first bit of rugby silverware I ever had – although unfortunately it was a loser's one. Dad was always encouraging me. He was very enthusiastic about my career, even at that tender age, and would invariably be there on the touchline cheering me on. But at no stage did I feel he was forcing me to play. It was a sort of gentle encouragement, just to keep me interested, though he was so keen that when I was 12 he made a special point of buying me a scrum-cap and, of all things, a jock-strap.

The mere fact that the scrum-cap was too big and I had nothing much to put into the jock-strap didn't seem to matter. Dad's attitude was that I'd grow into them anyway. My mother also used to come and watch me play, though Dad had to be around to keep her under control. It was a real embarrassment having Mum there because whenever she saw me tackled or with a bloodied nose, she was all for running on to the pitch and sorting out whoever had whacked me.

From the age of nine until I joined the police cadets my playing career was all Rugby League. I must have been reasonably good at it, too, because I went on to play for the town schools team at both junior and senior levels. I used to tune in to the Rugby Union internationals on television, of course, but although I enjoyed them the big thing was going down to Wilderspool to watch Warrington. It never dawned on me that one day I'd be out there at Twickenham following in the footsteps of Bill Beaumont. Bill was my England hero at that time, or so I like to make out. It would conjure up quite a picture to say I used to sit there in short pants watching him play; but anyone who looks up our respective ages will realise that such a scenario would have been impossible!

Educationally I was perhaps slightly above average and in my final year at junior school I was appointed head boy. However, I was never quite too sure why, because I seemed to spend a remarkable amount of time getting caned! Don't get the impression I was a rebel or had a reputation for getting into trouble. With my Dad being a policeman, I could not afford to be. It's just that Mr Horrocks was a strong believer in corporal punishment

The experimental three-tier education system operating in Warring-ton at the time was made up of secondary modern, secondary technical and grammar school components. My school, Beamont, was a secondary tech with the emphasis on subjects like physics, chemistry, metalwork and woodwork. Until my third year, when we amalgamated with the Oakwood girls school next door, it was an all-boys establishment and most of the lads went on to work for the electricity board or become gas fitters and the like.

The technical side didn't interest me because my natural inclination was to follow my father into the police force. Mind you, I was also keen on cooking and at one time had big designs on becoming a chef. In fact, Dad spent a considerable amount of time taking me around various hotels, restaurants, kitchens and hospitals to gather information on the subject.

I was always pretty tall for my age, but in my schooldays certainly not *the* tallest in the class. I clearly remember three or four monsters towering above me, including one boy called Bob Sinclair. Oddly enough

I met Bob again not so long ago . . . only these days the situation is somewhat different. He stopped growing at 6ft 5in and is now looking up at me!

In June 1974, four months before my 17th birthday, I left school with five O-levels (later to be followed after police training by a Sociology O-level and English A-level) and my mind finally made up to become a policeman. For the next few months I worked on a maintenance gang for my father's friend, local metal merchant Frankie Dunn, in order to earn enough money to tide me over until I could begin training as a cadet.

I might have been 6ft 4in tall but it was my first taste of a working environment, and grafting alongside some of the rough tattooed characters on the gang was quite an awakening for me. I think my Dad had even locked a couple of them up in the past, but for all that they still thought the world of him. Basically they were the salt of the earth, looking after each other . . . and indeed the young pup that had been thrust into their ranks. It all helped me to grow up – and at 17½ I joined the cadets.

Police training at Lancashire HQ in Hutton, near Preston, constituted an initial ten-month cadet course, with considerable emphasis placed on further education and character building. Apart from the studying, which culminated with O-level and A-level exams, the course included challenging outdoor activities like canoeing, mountaineering, abseiling and assault course work, along with the marching and drill-square work one finds in such an environment. Of course there was also a great deal of sport, including one game I had never played up to that point – Rugby Union.

We were 72 recruits in all, and when it came to dividing us into groups, I was appointed leader of one of the four sections. It was quite a responsibility for a youngster, new to such regimented surroundings, accompanying the course commander and drill sergeant on their regular Monday morning inspection tour. If anything was amiss it was my job to see it was put right, and for nine months I coped well with the added responsibility. Then, with just four weeks to go to the end of the course, I proceeded to get myself demoted!

Being teenagers, it was perhaps inevitable that youthful exuberance would at some stage get the better of disciplined restraint. However, that sort of behaviour was intolerable in a police training college, so when I decided to join in the revelry of a water battle with fire hoses between the two cadet blocks, rather than prevent it, there was only one possible course of action from my superiors. They took my lanyard off me and for the last month of the course I was reduced to the ranks.

After the passing out parade followed a six-month induction course, including a certain amount of time out on section. I found myself going round schools with a recruiting sergeant called Gerry Rothwell, encouraging other youngsters to join the force. Then came the big day when we were given our police uniforms and sworn in by a visiting magistrate. On 19 April 1976, I was appointed into the Lancashire Constabulary as PC 700, a number I actually selected myself and which I still hold to this day. Normally new constables have no say in such things, but as I had been working in the recruiting department I was in a somewhat privileged position. I actually wanted my father's old number, but since it was taken I flicked through the vacant ones . . . and opted to become a backward 007!

Throughout our training, quite a few of the cadets had been developing as Rugby Union players. We began as a hotch-potch of players thrown together, several of whom had never played the game before. Yet amazingly we clicked. We played against sixth-form colleges like Stonyhurst and Fleetwood Grammar School and during the entire ten-month cadet course lost just three games. We were, you might say, a force to be reckoned with.

I played at No. 8 and although the ball was the same shape I had been familiar with since my childhood in Latchford, the 15-man game was a totally new experience for me. During the 12 months after leaving school I shot up to 6ft 7in, but in terms of Rugby Union I was completely raw and had an awful lot to learn.

I was also a total beginner in the world of police work. My spell at Hutton was followed by ten weeks at the Home Office training school at Bruche, near Warrington, and I also underwent a driving course before finally being posted to the town I had requested . . . Blackpool. I particularly wanted to work in Britain's most popular holiday resort because I relished the idea of a posting amidst the bright lights and dazzling night life of the north-west's tourism capital; a resort through which several million holidaymakers passed every year.

Blackpool was an amazing place, and for that matter still is. I couldn't get over how busy it was in the summer season, so busy in fact that many's the time I've seen police cars forced to jockey with the trams on the tram-tracks because all four lanes of the promenade have been blocked. That was just normal weekend traffic, and it didn't end in September like any normal seaside resort. In Blackpool's case there were another couple of months of chaos to be dealt with, courtesy of the illuminations and all the action that went with them.

It was around seven o'clock one Monday morning in August 1976 that I sampled Blackpool's unique atmosphere for the first time. I was due at the police station at nine and there was no way I was going to arrive late. I must have set off in virtual darkness because by seven a.m. I was sitting outside the home of my landlady-to-be, Betty Stemp. There I was, accompanied by a dawn chorus of seagulls and roadsweepers, waiting for the good lady to wake up and let me in. I was to spend the next five years with Betty, her husband Jimmy and their crazy bull terrior Spike.

While Betty fitted perfectly into my image of a typical Blackpool landlady, Jimmy was an amazing fellow; a real character. Although he was a muscular, outgoing guy, there was also a sad side to his personality. One day he had been standing on the sea front when a local aerobatics daredevil buzzed the promenade in his plane. It was a manoeuvre they occasionally carried out, but which on this particular occasion had tragic consequences. When the low-flying aircraft screamed past poor Jimmy, it triggered a frightening reaction in his subconscious, and from that day until his death he was afflicted by chronic agoraphobia. As a result, he simply could not bring himself to go any distance from his own doorstep. It meant he and Betty could never go away on holiday; and he was limited to working as a steward in the Brunswick Club at the end of the street.

Spike was Jimmy's pride and joy, a complete lunatic of an animal which liked nothing better than to terrorise the unsuspecting young policemen Betty took in as lodgers. I quickly came to terms with the dog's aggression; but if any of the other boys showed the slightest sign of weakness, the muzzled mutt would be down on them like a ton of bricks. A knock on the door was the signal for Spike to go berserk. He'd tear down the hall, launch himself at the front door, and woe betide anyone who got in the way.

It was a common sight to see a bewildered colleague pinned to his chair under four stone of canine muscle. That problem never bothered me, however, because I had made my peace with Spike early on. It's amazing what a wrestle and a roll on the floor could do in helping to bypass his special brand of initiation ceremony.

As the tallest bobby in the town, I was obviously pretty conspicuous – particularly as I'm around 7ft 2in tall wearing a helmet. Although that may sound pretty daunting, it's a fact that the bigger policemen are generally the easiest-going guys. As a result some people think they can get away with things; and occasionally they do. One such example was the only villain who ever hurt me in the course of my duty.

I had received an assistance call to go to Talbot Square, where trouble had broken out after people had spilled out of the pubs and clubs. When I got there, one of the policemen on my shift was in the middle of the crowd struggling with two men against the wall of a bank. He had his arm round one and was hanging on to the other for grim life – a huge guy, even taller than me. Since the two of them had obviously been misbehaving in some way, I went to my colleague's assistance by trying to grab the big fellow. He promptly swung his arm round and split my lip. Trying to keep calm, I made another grab for him and as I did so he disappeared. Totally bewildered, I looked down at the ground . . . into the pleading eyes of a tiny guy cowering at my feet. This was no giant of a man after all. He had merely been doing his fighting standing on the bench outside the bank! I mean, how could a 6ft 8in cop drag a bloke of 5ft 2in in to the desk sergeant and say: 'This guy's just burst my lip, sarge'? So I gave the little nuisance a kick up the backside and sent him packing down the street.

In those early days, Blackpool in some ways was a bit like Dodge City. I had never experienced pub fights before and some of them were right out of the Wild West films, just like the saloon-bar brawls you see on the screen. Sometimes we would get to the door but just couldn't go in to sort out the trouble. Bottles, chairs, tables, doormen, all sorts of things would be flying all over the place and the only way to avoid being hurt yourself was to wait and let the trouble die down before taking action.

During Scottish weeks, the Scots authorities would send down their own policemen to identify troublemakers from north of the border. Very often the bobbies would be on hand at pub fights involving Scots to point out the ringleaders to us. Along with the town's Wakes Weeks, those Scots weekends and fortnights were always lively affairs. But pub trouble has decreased dramatically in recent years and while Blackpool is still a busy town during the season – and to my mind as fine a family resort as you can find anywhere in Europe – it is certainly quieter than during my early days on the beat.

When it comes to dealing with violent situations as a policeman, I have always adopted the 'softly softly' approach my father taught me. The important concept is never to rush in, just walk calmly up to the problem and more often than not the situation resolves itself. In my opinion it is still the best policy and it usually works.

One occasion which tested my nerve to the full was a major outbreak of violence at a football match some years ago. It came completely out of the blue and was one of the few occasions on which I have been genuinely frightened for my safety. The game was a Second Division encounter between Blackpool and Stoke watched by a 26,000 crowd at Bloomfield Road on a beautiful day – and trouble was the last thing I and my police colleagues were expecting. Suddenly, as a few bobbies went into the Kop to stop Stoke fans climbing on the front fence, the place erupted. With the police on the Kop engulfed, we moved in to rescue them and were promptly attacked from all sides. In the riot situation that followed I was forced to draw my staff for the only time in my career in order to defend myself. I was punched, kicked and spat at and it really was a case of fighting for survival; all that mattered was getting myself and my colleagues out safely. Later there were more problems as the trouble-makers smashed up the ground and nearby hotels, and even resorted to turning over police cars. It was a relief to survive it all unharmed, and when I got home everything was brought home to me. As I sat at the tea table, I realised my hands were shaking.

Overall, my first few years of police service proved to be quite an experience, with visits to Toxteth and Moss Side during the troubles . . . and all points north, south, east and west during the miners' strike.

My rugby career was coming on all the time, and I soon graduated, via the Blackpool Division, to the Lancashire Police team. The county side has since developed into a pretty mean outfit, but at that time it was just social rugby. Sometimes we would turn up with only 11 men and fitness was something that used to come in phases. It was a case of working hard and playing hard and as we spent a lot of time socialising we felt we had to do a bit of training to balance it out. Nowadays I train a lot on my own but in those days I had difficulty motivating myself, so over the course of a season my fitness would go up and down like a yo-yo. I also used to keep in trim playing volleyball and soccer for a Blackpool pub side. As you might expect I wasn't bad in the air for a centre-half . . . and could put in a pretty mean tackle, too!

I'd had a pretty good grounding in the game . . . on the big playing field at the back of our house in Latchford. There were two or three football pitches just under the railway embankment, and 20 or 30 of us would rush down there straight from school and spend forever kicking a ball about.

Since some of my police colleagues were playing at Fylde I drifted down there for a while, never getting really involved and slumming around in the third team. What with my new job and the Blackpool social scene, rugby was not particularly important to me. As a result I never made the first team and missed the chance to play alongside Billy Beaumont. It is still one of my greatest regrets that I didn't have the opportunity to turn out with or against England's 1980 Grand Slam captain. In those days I only saw Bill at Fylde occasionally because of his England commitments, in much the way they were to dominate my life at Preston Grasshoppers a few years later. But when he was there he would make a point of coming over for a chat with the new boys. That's the type of true club man Bill was and still is.

However, Fylde was not really my scene, and after some six months there I was playing for Lancashire Police against Preston when Grasshoppers committee man Pym Simons, who later became club president, invited me to play for them. I wasn't keen on the idea but the powers of persuasion of the Aged P, as Sharon affectionately calls him, are legendary. Predictably I finished up saying yes . . . and it was to be one of the most important decisions of my life.

CHAPTER FOUR

One Giant Hop

AS introductions go, my first game for Preston Grasshoppers was not exactly awe-inspiring. I was 19½, and it was an evening game against an army touring side. Since I was on leave from the police I drove over from Warrington only to get lost on the motorway. I might have guessed even then that it was not going to be my night – but worse was to follow. I had to make a detour after finding myself on the M55 heading for Blackpool and when I finally arrived at the Hoppers ground a harassed offical met me at the gate and ushered me through the club into the changing-room. The game had already started so I stripped off and got changed in double-quick time, dashed out on to the touchline in my tracksuit, and with questionable enthusiasm awaited the call.

One of the Preston players immediately threw himself to the ground, his motive somewhat unclear. I'm convinced he wasn't really hurt so I can only assume he was either very eager to get off or relieved to see me on the touchline. My big moment had come. As he was carried from the pitch I stripped off and rather reluctantly entered the affray.

Ten minutes later I was following the same route on a stretcher, having received a knock in the back and a dislodged vertebrae for my pains. How it came about I had no idea, but obviously I had been somewhere I shouldn't have been! In fact, for all I knew the damage might even have been done by one of my own players.

Needless to say we were comprehensively beaten and I was laid up in extreme pain for three weeks, stretched out on a board keeping as still as possible. Eventually I had to consult an osteopath because I simply could not move.

However, any negative thoughts I had about rugby wore off once I got mobile again, even though I certainly was not the easiest of players to motivate. I had never been involved at senior level before and it was flattering that Hoppers wanted me in their first team. Having said that, if I could find a way to avoid playing I would. A combination of living in a new town, enjoying my new job and revelling in the social life that accompanied it added to the motivation problem. Any excuse would do because I just wasn't 100 per cent into the idea of playing serious rugby week in, week out. Consequently it was some months before I drifted back down to the club and resumed my Preston playing career.

I certainly wasn't going to play the weekend England travelled to Murrayfield to face Scotland for the 1980 Grand Slam. I had never been to a rugby international before, so when I managed to get a ticket there was no way club rugby was going to interfere with such a momentous occasion. Billy Beaumont's boys were on the brink of a Five Nations clean sweep for the first time in 23 years, so when Grasshoppers officials asked me to play in a Merit Table game against Wakefield on the same day, it was no contest. Declaring myself unavailable for selection due to work commitments would just about cover it . . . or so I thought.

When the big day dawned, several of the Hoppers boys jumped into a couple of cars and, armed with our overnight bags, drove up to Hawick where we booked into an hotel. Then on we went to Edinburgh and the hostelries along Princes Street. The atmosphere was amazing, the two sets of supporters mingling happily in the unique spirit of cameraderie that typifies rugby internationals. The pubs were jam-packed with fans of both persuasions. We had been knocking the pints back for some time and preparing ourselves for the feast of rugby to come when one of the boys, ever alert to the unpredictable, suddenly announced: 'Look out there – it's the Grasshoppers bus!'

Sure enough, there was the Preston club coach stuck in the snail of traffic outside the pub. We all dashed out into Princes Street, pint pots raised high in the air, and gave the boys a rousing chorus as the bus crawled past. It simply hadn't dawned on me in my celebratory mood that the club officials also had better things to do than involve themselves in a Merit Table game. Chief selector Andy Proctor looked out at me, I gazed back . . . and the following week I found myself dropped to the fifth team! I still had the last laugh, however, because that fifth-team trip to Upper Eden in the Lake District was one of the most entertaining rugby outings I have ever had. I played at No. 8, scored three tries and had a field day on the park. Then it was on to the sleepy little market town of Kirby Stephen, and a splendid night's entertainment at one of the local hostelries. I finally arrived home at four a.m. considerably the worse for wear. What a punishment! Coarse rugby at its very best!

As well as playing for Grasshoppers I was also turning out for

Lancashire Police on a Wednesday. I had been playing for the police on and off since I was a senior cadet, both in the county and the Blackpool divisional team. Nowadays Lancashire are among the best sides in the British force, even if we are still waiting to win the national Police Cup despite reaching the final six times in eight years! It is all part of the force policy to encourage police officers to participate in sport; to get them involved in the communities and the areas in which they work. It also breaks up the day-to-day routine and stress of police work – not to mention providing an ideal means of winding down and keeping fit.

The turning point for both Grasshoppers and myself came with the arrival in 1979 of Dick Greenwood as player-coach. Dick, a former Waterloo player who was later to take over as England coach, was himself capped four times as a flanker in the '60s and skippered the team against Ireland in 1969. Some 12 months before he joined Preston I actually played against him for Lancashire Police at Blackburn, although I must admit my recollections of that day are extremely vague. Dick clearly has a much better memory than me, because in a newspaper article a couple of years ago he described that first meeting in the following terms:

'I left the dressing-room to go outside for my nervous pre-match visit to the gents. A nice day, then all of a sudden the sun went out as if there had been a total eclipse. I looked up and found this enormous youth standing next to me. I went back into the dressing-room, and said, "Do we have to play against this fellow?" I then made my second visit to the gents.'

Dick also reckons he had to bully me into taking my rugby seriously. Well, bullying might be too strong a word but as I have already said I was definitely not as dedicated to the game as I should have been.

Gradually, however, rugby was coming to the fore. Away from Preston, the Lancashire Police side also took on a new image with a lot of the older heads drifting away and the youngsters (the majority of whom played their weekend club rugby at Grasshoppers anyway) starting to take over. We were playing well, winning often – and the more successful we were, the more we wanted to play. It was a bit of a bug really.

My first major representative game was for the English Police against the Welsh at Nottingham. The call came not long after I had met my wife-to-be Sharon, and I felt distinctly honoured. On a filthy day, I took the field bursting with pride, only to get my come-uppance from the strongest opposition I had yet faced. To my despair, the result was as bad as the weather.

Sharon and I had met in the police after our initial training period. Her family moved up to Southport from Harrow when she was ten years old and after leaving school she joined the Merseyside Police, the Lancashire force's next-door neighbours. We met on a continuation course at Hutton after our initial training period. The date was 9 January 1978, so Sharon reminds me, and eight days later we went on our first date – to a quaint country pub in the beautiful Trough of Bowland. Very romantic, I thought. I must have impressed her because all she remembers is that I kept smacking my head on the beams! Six weeks later, on a night out at the El Tonel wine bar in Southport, I proposed; and on 25 October 1980 we were married at St Cuthbert's Church in Churchtown, near Southport.

Most normal couples jet off for a romantic break after their wedding – but not us. We didn't honeymoon due to Lancashire's appearance in the quarter-final of the national Police Cup against the Royal Ulster Constabulary at Preston. The consolation was that we went on to reach the final and it was the start of Sharon's long-term commitment to my rugby career, for better or worse.

Meanwhile, my rugby limitations were really brought home to me when I was selected for the British Police against an International XV. I found myself on the same field as veteran Welsh locks Bob Penberthy and Allan Martin, two of the legends of the valleys. I jumped against Penberthy and had the audacity to pinch the first lineout ball off the big man from Pontypridd. From then on he put me through the mill, but I must have made some impression on him because in the clubhouse afterwards I suddenly felt a slap on the back – and he insisted on buying me a drink.

England's Grand Slam win in 1980 had a big impact on me. Apart from helping to bring about that splendid punishment in the Lake District, it hooked me on the game and from then on my career seemed to improve by leaps and bounds. Greenwood, of course, was the prime motivator and he spent a lot of time working on my game and encouraging me. I have always had a lot of time for Dick's training methods and he was brimming with good ideas on fitness. He soon turned Grasshoppers into quite a force in the north west, so much so that we twice reached the Lancashire Cup final, beating top teams like Orrell and Waterloo on the way. In fact, at one point we were one of the best sides in the north, without ever receiving the recognition we deserved.

There were no real stars at Grasshoppers. Fellow forwards Stan Sherlock, Mick Billington, Brent Horton, Neil Leeming, Alan Wyllie, Roy Dransfield and Micky Parker, most of whom had developed through the Colts side, were all part and parcel of our success and we grew up together as a team. Like myself, Wyllie and Parker also went on to achieve representative honours with Lancashire.

In 1982 I had my first experience of playing abroad . . . on a highly enjoyable club tour of Canada. We played in Ottawa and Toronto, and it paved the way for further exotic Hoppers trips, including a three-centre tour of the Cayman Islands, Miami and Florida.

Preston's success on the field had a snowball effect because as the team improved, so did my own game. With their success I became increasingly keen to get down to the club and be involved in it all. Along with that little bit of success on the field, I was also enjoying the social side of things, making a lot of close friends at the club and generally enjoying the family atmosphere.

For two or three seasons I looked no further rugby-wise than playing for Grasshoppers and the British Police. Then, early in 1983, I was selected for Lancashire B – my first representative game outside the police. To be recognised at county level filled me with pride. It was a special honour, an ideal I had always cherished; and to this day my Lancashire caps are among my proudest memories next to playing for England and the British Lions.

My introduction to representative rugby was somewhat bizarre to say the least. Three days before the Lancashire B clash with Cumbria I was playing for Preston against Kendal, and up against a guy called John Veivers. As things would have it we found ourselves swinging punches toe-to-toe at a lineout . . . and I was sent off for the only time in my career.

It wasn't that I was entirely the guilty party, just that Veivers happened to be flat on his back at the time! As luck would have it, he got up and was allowed to play on while I, being deemed the guilty party for no other reason than that I remained on my feet, was banned for four weeks. It was no consolation to me that one of the Kendal props was also sent off and as I soaked myself in the bath, feeling sorry for myself and rueing the representative honour that had just gone begging, it seemed I had blown my Lancashire chances for the season. Not that

my Preston team-mate Alan Wyllie was complaining because it was he
who took my place in the Lancashire B side.

Later, Veivers and I had a beer in the bar together and patched up
our differences in time-honoured rugby tradition. For all the bitterness
out on the pitch, once the game is over it is all forgotten – be it a
meaningless friendly or a World Cup final.

I eventually made my Lancashire B debut against Yorkshire at
Headingley on 8 March 1983. It was a strong Lancashire team, too,
containing quality players like Orrell's Simon Langford, Neil Hitchen
and Bob Kimmins. Yet although I was new to the county scene, I found
little difficulty slotting in. It was not as if I had no experience of
competing with players of that standard; in fact I could number full
internationals like Welshmen Steve Sutton and Alun Donovan among
my colleagues in the British Police team.

The following season I won my first senior cap for the county –
against Eastern Counties. It was the fulfilment of any Lancashire lad's
ambition, and it threw me in with a great bunch of lads and an excellent
side as well. I quickly gained from the experience of playing with people
like Sammy Southern, Jim Syddall and Phil Moss. Indeed, after England's
Paul Rendall, Sammy was one of the best No. 3 lineout exponents in the
game. He had honed his support play on his jumpers to a fine art and in the
next few years I learnt a considerable amount from him and Syddall.

After jumping the Lancashire hurdle pretty successfully, I then
found myself in contention for an even greater honour; selection for the
North. But once again, as with my first Lancashire B appearance, fate
was to rob me of my initial chance.

That year, 1984, was disrupted by the miners' strike which meant
I spent long periods away from home. Sometimes I'd be on picket duty
in South Yorkshire or Derbyshire for five, six, even seven days on the
trot, holed up in a police van and working all sorts of crazy hours. And
right in the middle of it I was called up for the North's October game
against Ulster.

A few days later I was sitting in a van at some unearthly hour
reading the early editions of the Sunday papers when I spotted the
headline: 'DOOLEY'S TOP OF THE WANTED LIST'. The article
began: 'The choice of the North team to play Ulster this week as a
prelude to their match against the Australians has been greeted with
wide approval. But one question is "Who is Wade Dooley?".' The same
question was still being asked after the Ulster game . . . because I didn't
play. This time I broke my thumb playing for Hoppers, an injury that

also cost me a place on the bench against Andy Slack's all-conquering Australians the following month. But I did have one small consolation – my name actually appeared in the programme!

Despite my injury, I wasn't forgotten by the powers-that-be and was again picked on the bench for the clash with Romania a few weeks later. I did not make a particularly good impression with team manager Mike Weston because I didn't turn up for either of the pre-match training sessions. The first time the weather was so treacherous that I decided to give it a miss, only to discover later that the other boys had made it. Then, when the squad got together the day before the game, I had to opt out because I was on duty.

I finally joined up with the team a couple of hours before the match and Weston immediately rounded on me. In front of everyone in the Birkenhead Park clubhouse, he told me in no uncertain manner that if I continued to show such lack of commitment I could forget about representative rugby there and then. While I did not like the way he chose to bawl me out, I could hardly complain at the dressing down. My attitude had been wrong, but I discovered in the light of subsequent events that Mike was not a man to hold grudges. That was just as well, because he was to become England's next chairman of selectors. I actually spent the first hour of the game freezing to death in the stand. The weather was awful and when Syddall tweaked a hamstring I was not exactly straining at the leash to go out and replace him. Anyway, I fully expected him to finish the game, even when I was told to get stretched off.

Somewhat unenthusiastically, I trundled down to the touchline and was going through the motions when the ball was booted out of play. I happened to catch it – and within a couple of weeks that incident was to become a prize BBC archive. Moments later, Jim hobbled out of the action with the injury that was to cost him his England place and on I went for the last 20 minutes. Although we won the game, there was no way I could prove myself in such miserable conditions; it was hard enough trying to keep the rain and the mud out of my eyes.

As for the Romanians, they quickly drowned their sorrows by drinking the place dry after the game. The oppression of the Ceausescu regime must have made the buffet and drinks laid out in the Birkenhead Park squash courts look like a royal banquet to them. There were bottles of spirits everywhere, and while the English boys were supping pints, most of the Romanians began lacing into the whisky . . . by the tumbler-ful! Then the bottles started to go missing, and by the time the reception ended virtually everything seemed to have been spirited away, no doubt to find its way in due course into some peasant home in Bucharest. As for the Romanian players themselves, they had knocked back so much drink so quickly that most of them were paralytic!

Although I knew Dick Greenwood was involved in the England set-up I hadn't even given a thought to the possibility of being picked for the England v Romania game. England had been well beaten by Australia a few weeks earlier and I knew there might be changes. I had watched Syddall and 20-year-old Nigel Redman given a torrid time by the Wallaby second row and as I sat in front of the TV I remember thinking that, given a chance, I might well be able to do something at that level. Yet despite their growing injury list and my 20 minutes wallowing in the mud for the North, I certainly had no inkling I might be called up.

On New Year's Day, 1985, I was back on an eight p.m. to four a.m. night duty with the divisional support unit, sitting with three colleagues in the office before going out on duty, when someone phoned for me. 'This is Terry Cooper of the Press Association,' said the voice. 'You've been selected for England. Any reaction?' Reaction? I nearly fell off my chair laughing.

Poor Terry must have wondered what hit him because I gave him the brush-off in no mean terms and put the phone down – just as Sharon had done when he phoned her at home a few minutes earlier. Well aware that policemen and rugby players are probably the world's biggest wind-up merchants, I looked around the office to see which of the boys was behind this particular micky-take.

Then I thought no more of it until the phone rang again. It sounded like a party was going on in the background as Hoppers secretary Les Anson announced: 'Someone has just rung up from Twickenham. You've been picked for England.' This time I knew it was no wind-up. The call from Cooper really had been genuine and I was just four days from becoming a fully-fledged England international. The enthusiasm at the Preston club was only natural. After all, the last of their five previous internationals, J. A. Scholfield, won his one and only England cap way back in 1911!

From then on the phone just did not stop. It really was instant fame as the media caught up with the story. Journalists, family, people from the club, friends, it was sheer bedlam. So chaotic in fact that eventually I had to tell the switchboard: 'No more calls. I was supposed to go out on duty two hours ago.' Eventually I managed to get out, leaving bemused communications room staff to log the calls that were still flooding in.

My shock was evident from the comments I made to the press at the time: 'I'm dumbfounded,' I was quoted as saying. 'It was right out of the blue and I'll have to ask my sergeant for time off.' Despite England's injury problems, I had been sure other players were ahead of me in the queue. It seemed that everyone else must have been suspended or just didn't fit the bill. In the event, the England selectors had made 11 changes and brought in six new caps, Simon Smith, Rob Andrew, Richard Harding, Kevin Simms, John Orwin and myself. And I was the biggest surprise of all.

At four a.m., work on the support unit over for the night, I was in no mood for sleeping so out I went with a few of the boys for a celebratory 'choir practice'. To the uninitiated, that's police parlance for a few pints. The upshot of it all was that I finally arrived home some time after seven – just in time to say good morning to Sharon as she left for work!

It must have been around eight when I got to bed . . . only to be woken two hours later by a phone call from work saying the Press wanted to speak to me. When I got up and looked out, a reporter and cameraman were camped on the doorstep. How they got my address I'll never know but after a quick photo session, assisted by my pet Airedale dog Janna, it was off to the station to be met by the TV and Press corps. Minutes later the cameras were clicking away merrily as I ran along Blackpool sands in full uniform, rugby ball tucked under my arm and attempting to balance my helmet on my head.

When BBC's *Grandstand* decided to spotlight the new caps in their build-up to the game, they had no trouble digging out footage of the other players, but all they could find of me was that clip catching the ball as I stretched off at Birkenhead Park. So they spotlighted it, put a ring around my head and told the world: this is England's new lock Wade Dooley. I was on TV for the first time.

I was in a strange, totally new world, but in the light of later experiences the England camp at that time was certainly not the best-organised of set-ups. These days players and their spouses are so well looked after that even the wives receive personal letters from the RFU ladies' representative Carmen McDonald sorting out individual arrangements before and after each game. Quite rightly, too, because you are playing for your country after all. Yet back in 1985 new caps were not even told they needed a dinner suit for the after-match banquet.

I realised there might be some sort of reception after the game, but I had no idea it was a black-tie job; in any case I had never worn that sort of gear in my life. As the big day neared Sharon happened to be talking to Roger Uttley's sister in Blackpool when she discovered by chance that there was an official formal dinner. When she was told she would need an evening dress and I a dinner suit, that was the signal for blind panic.

Where was I, at 6ft 8in and 18 stone, going to get a dinner suit at a few days' notice? I mean, there was no way I could buy one off the peg and nowhere near enough time to get one made. Fortunately one of my colleagues at work came to the rescue by offering to lend me his. The only problem was that he was three or four inches shorter than me – and a bit more rounded too. But at least it was a dinner suit and thanks to some judicious pinning in strategic places by Sharon I managed to get by, even if the trousers weren't long enough and the sleeves too short. As it was, I finished up looking more like an out-of-work wine waiter than an international rugby player and under strict instructions from the wife *not* to take the jacket off under any circumstances.

My first problem when I got down to England headquarters in Richmond on the Thursday was to find someone I knew! Jim Syddall, my only contact in the team, had pulled out with a recurrence of the hamstring injury he suffered playing for the North and my only real contact was Dick Greenwood. Rob Andrew, Rory Underwood and Kevin Simms were all playing for the North at the time, but I hardly knew them since I had only just come on to the divisional scene, let alone the international set-up. They didn't know me either, and in fact skipper Paul Dodge started referring to me as 'Wayne' in his pre-match interviews. In the event it was Gloucester prop Phil Blakeway who took me under his wing, gave me valuable advice and helped me to feel at home among what were, after all, a bunch of strangers. Very grateful I was for it, too. I also hit it off straight away with players like Steve Brain and Gary Pearce, but that doesn't mean the others didn't make me welcome. The difference was that whereas they were all involved in the same first-class club scene, I had suddenly arrived on the international stage from nowhere.

John Orwin eventually arrived from Gloucester to replace Syddall as my second-row partner and we had just two days' training at St Mary's College to develop a playing pattern together. It was quite a challenge trying to fit in with people I had never met before, let alone played with.

On the big day I woke at six a.m., three hours before breakfast. Big-match nerves were beginning to get to me. Later in the morning the pressure eased somewhat when Dick took us for what was at that time a customary walk along the Thames . . . but now I felt apprehension taking over, particularly with so many new faces in the side.

Then it was on to Twickenham. As the team coach drove on to the West Car Park, which as ever was crowded with supporters enjoying car-boot barbecues, the jokes were flying thick and fast among the players. Bob Hesford stood up in the aisle and made a special point of identifying me for the benefit of the fans milling around the bus. 'Wade Dooley, Preston Grasshoppers,' he announced theatrically, gesturing in my direction. It was a light-hearted moment, and Bob's way of easing the tension for the new players. It worked, too.

My family and a crowd of Preston players and committee men were waiting for me outside the players' entrance, armed with an enormous club banner. I felt almost like being at home as I made my way into the inner sanctum, expecting to find the most luxurious of modern changing-rooms. Instead, I walked into a splendidly archaic set-up that was to become so familiar over the next eight seasons. The old-fashioned wood panelling, big cast-iron baths and frosted-glass windows came as something of a surprise initially, but the place oozed character and in later years I felt remarkably comfortable within its unique ancient walls. Behind the frosted windows I could see the shadows of supporters and hear their shouting and laughing as they stood outside, blissfully unaware that the people they had come to see were preparing for battle literally inches away. I was soon to discover that there's no other international ground quite like it.

My England shirt was hanging on the peg that was to become such familiar territory, with my shorts and socks laid out, and a mountain of mail alongside. As a player's appearances mount, the congratulatory letters and cards tend to dwindle – but new caps are invariably swamped with them. I made a point of reading them all, then strolled out for a quick pitch inspection. We had been down to take a look at the ground 24 hours earlier, but this time it didn't look quite so enormous. A quick check on the surface told me it was right for a long stud . . . which was just as well because I didn't possess any others!

The moment I took the field with my new team-mates for that first England game is something I wanted to savour for ever. Twickenham was only half-full, yet the buzz and the passion of running out in front of 30,000 people was indescribable. To me the atmosphere seemed electric, which was hardly surprising since the crowd was ten times as big as anything I had experienced before. Pride and emotion took over as the anthems were played, and then came a huge sense of relief as the game kicked off. My England debut was under way . . . and suddenly the crowd and the razzamatazz had reached into another world.

The match itself was the fastest game I'd ever played in. After 30 frenetic minutes in which I gave it a real blast it was just a matter of hanging on for grim life. The fitness level just wasn't there and as John Mason wrote in the *Daily Telegraph* the following Monday: 'Dooley's legs, after a commendable first hour, turned to rubber . . .'

Nevertheless, I was quite pleased overall with my debut performance. Apart from the fact that we won 22–15, I had gained a reasonable amount of lineout possession, made a couple of encouraging runs and done some useful work in the loose play. I also managed to hang on to my first-ever England jersey in somewhat bizarre fashion despite my opposite number Gheorghe Caragea's eagerness to swop. I desperately wanted to keep my own shirt as a souvenir of my debut and Phil Blakeway, who had been through it all before in 15 previous internationals, came to my aid by giving me his to exchange. It was a gesture I greatly appreciated because it left me not only with my own jersey, which is now proudly housed in a showcase at home, but also with Caragea's.

The selectors were sufficiently impressed to re-select me for the Five Nations opener against France, but in my heart of hearts I knew I was nowhere near fit enough to compete effectively at that level. There was a full month before the French game, so I launched myself into the task of getting myself fit. Fortunately my police partner at the time, Alan Todd, was a fitness fanatic and for four weeks we trained together frantically on the Blackpool sand dunes. It was eyeballs-out stuff, and it paid off because against France I found it much easier to keep up with the pace. And since then, strange though it may seem to some, I have never had any problem stepping up from junior club rugby to full-scale internationals.

Looking back, Australia and New Zealand were so far ahead of us at that time largely because the England players weren't half as fit as they should have been. Even though Dick Greenwood was heavily into fitness, not many of the England players were in proper condition for international rugby. Indeed, it was only when Geoff Cooke arrived on the scene as manager that professional fitness experts came into the picture and England's fortunes started to change.

That year we had a particularly bad winter and a number of Five Nations games were postponed, including the one against Wales in Cardiff. That match was eventually put back to the middle of April, which left me in the fortunate position of playing my first three internationals at Twickenham – against Romania, France and Scotland.

There were 62,000 in the ground for the French game, the largest crowd I'd ever seen, and I clearly remember standing there singing the national anthem with a lump in my throat. I am not a particularly emotional person, but it is easy to understand why players are so affected by their country's anthems. Why, for instance, Welsh fullback Paul Thorburn in later years would stand with tears streaming down his face and England's Simon Hodgkinson kiss the rose on his shirt. And why French jaws also quivered as the strains of the *Marseillaise* rang out.

It was hard to believe I was actually on the same field as world-class stars like Serge Blanco, Philippe Sella and even my opposite number Jean Condom. We were heavy underdogs against the odds-on Championship favourites, most of the so-called experts having tipped us to finish bottom of the heap. Yet we turned in a performance that surprised everyone, not least the French, with Orwin, Hesford and myself cleaning out Condom, Francis Haget and Co in the lineout. Thanks to Rob Andrew, who kicked two penalties and a dropped goal to add to the 18 points he scored on his debut against Romania, we forced a 9–9 draw. We could have won, too, had Simon Smith not put a foot in touch as he dived for the line in a last-ditch effort to snatch the game. Yet on reflection it was probably a fair result, since France were robbed of a certain try when Richard Harding's despairing tackle knocked the ball out of Patrick Esteve's hands just as the flying French wing was grounding the ball.

This time I was completely happy with my performance. So was Bill Beaumont, who gave me a rave notice in his *Rugby World* column, saying: 'It's difficult to single out individuals on the England side, but I thought Dooley had a great game, and is really proving an inspired choice and a wise gamble on the part of the selectors.'

The only problem after that match was that I could not communicate with the opposition because I don't speak a word of French! Condom and I found ourselves on a table together, along with a couple of committee men: and there we sat, nodding and smiling at each other, yet unable to exchange a single word! The French have a much better system. At team dinners in Paris they put all their own players on one big table at one end of the room and the opposition at the other end.

I had still not experienced defeat in an England shirt after the next game, a 10–7 Calcutta Cup win over Scotland. This time I found myself facing stars like John Rutherford, Colin Deans, David Leslie, Iain Paxton and my opposite number Alan Tomes, all of whom had experienced the joy of winning the Grand Slam the previous year. It was a challenge I savoured, and our victory completed the ultimate embarrassment for the Scots of plummeting from Grand Slam to Championship whitewash inside 12 months.

I was finding the pace easier all the time, largely because I was working a lot harder in training. I was also getting a little more streetwise with every game, and two wins and a draw in my first three inter-nationals, particularly at a time when England were in something of a turmoil, was more than I could have hoped for. It had also given us a chance of winning the Championship when at the start of the year no one thought we had a prayer.

It couldn't last, of course, and it finally came apart when we lost 13–10 to eventual champions Ireland at Lansdowne Road. But what an experience my first trip to Dublin turned out to be! It all started with an amazing coach journey, complete with police outriders, from the airport to our hotel in Killiney. The security was particularly tight in a happy Garda sort of way, but what a haphazard frolic the trip from the airport was as we roared through the centre of Dublin at speeds of 70 and 80mph. The boys all loved it.

At the hotel and our training HQ at Blackrock, the hospitality and food were out of this world. I reckon that's the Irish philosophy for beating the opposition – stuff them full of food and kill them with kindness. They would give us Mars bars with every meal and we'd finish up waddling out of the restaurant two stone heavier and hardly able to walk!

The Irish people could not have been friendlier . . . until we got on to the pitch, that is. That game was my toughest test yet, the day I discovered that when it comes to rugby you wear the Irish like a rash.

From the start Willie Anderson, Donal Lenihan and Phil Matthews swarmed all over me – and got away with it. These guys were more streetwise than any I'd played against, so unorthodox in everything they did. In fact, there was so much going on in the lineout you just couldn't keep track of it. In the end we lost 13–10 to a late dropped goal by Michael Kiernan and Ireland went on to win the Triple Crown. I was gutted, mainly because we had played well, certainly up front, and might easily have won.

But the disappointment was soon forgotten in the wake of the glorious evening that followed. I was about to learn that in Ireland the result is irrelevant. Win, lose or draw they celebrate in style . . . and that night at the Shelbourne Hotel was as good as any I've had in rugby. The hotel foyer was absolutely heaving with rugby fans and every time a player left the dinner and descended the long, winding staircase a huge round of applause would break out as he was swallowed up into the crowd. That night was also the first time I sampled Willie Anderson's special way of celebrating.

Basically anyone on Willie's table had to do what Willie wanted. And that was to drink . . . and drink . . . and drink. The big Ulsterman was so heavily into drinking games that anyone assigned to his table would try desperately to move elsewhere by switching the place-names before Willie arrived. But on this occasion we were paired up by playing positions – and I was fated to experience the Anderson excesses first-hand. The last thing I remember is Willie towering above me, dancing on the table . . . and the table collapsing. Food, plates, glasses, cutlery and candelabra crashed to the floor, followed closely by 16st 5lb of Irish second-row beef. I'm not sure where I was at the time; more than likely I was under the table. All I knew was that I'd never drunk so much. The next thing I remember is waking up under a chair in the club below our team hotel, still wearing my now-dishevelled dinner suit and clutching a half-empty bottle of champagne. I looked at my watch. In ten minutes we were due to depart for the airport. Frantically I dashed to my room, threw my things together and scrambled on to the coach . . . my head spinning and vowing to have a ten-gallon bladder fitted before the next trip to Dublin.

The overwhelming friendship I experienced in Ireland was in stark contrast to our final Five Nations game, the trip to Cardiff to face Wales in the game postponed from January. I had been to the Arms Park a couple of times to watch England, but as a player I suddenly found myself in a different type of environment . . . open hostility.

I have never experienced such a partisan crowd and things were to become far worse two years later. However, in 1985 we hadn't won at Cardiff for 22 years and despite our encouraging form through the season we weren't really expected to do it this time, either.

It was the day I came up for the first time against the man who was to prove my most difficult opponent, Bob Norster. We hit it off immediately in a love-hate relationship that was to run for years. Basically we loved to hate each other on the field; and we didn't spend too much time together off it, either. I never found Bob an easy man to get on with, yet as a lineout jumper he was the best technician I have ever come across and the only opponent I never came out on top of. For a man of only 6ft 5in he was extremely athletic and had his timing off to a fine art.

Very tall men like myself rely chiefly on our height and being able to get off the ground to win lineout ball. But Norster's lack of inches meant he had to be a bit more technical about it. His timing with his thrower and the support play around him were crucial aspects of his play; and over the years I was to have some disastrous afternoons against him. It was all the more satisfying, therefore, when I got the better of him with the British Lions in Australia in 1989 by ousting him from the team after the First Test.

That first meeting in 1985 ended up pretty even, which for an upstart like me coming out of junior club rugby was quite an achievement. I just tried to close down Norster's space as much as possible, get across him and make life generally difficult for him. We started to fall out there and then . . .

I also had good reason to remember the lad making his debut for Wales at stand-off. At one point Rob Andrew kicked a 22-metre drop-out short into centre field, and as Norster waited to collect it I hurtled through on the charge and steamed towards the half-way line. With the Welsh cover racing across desperately to stop me, I had visions of dashing 70 yards to score a sensational try. Suddenly I was confronted by this slip of a fly-half – and despite my attempt to run straight through him he managed to put me on the deck.

That was my introduction to a highly talented player who was obviously destined for greater things. His name was Jonathan Davies.

CHAPTER FIVE

All Black and Blue

I COULD hardly complain at my first season in international rugby, even if it did end on a losing note with the defeats in Dublin and Cardiff. I had the consolation of being voted Personality of the Year by the northern rugby writers and an extra bonus followed . . . a place in the England squad for the summer tour to New Zealand.

The itinerary was a testing one, to say the least. Seven games in three weeks, including two full Tests against the All Blacks plus a date with Auckland, the world's top provincial side, that would effectively be a third Test. But we certainly did not expect the 'welcome' the anti-apartheid movement had in store for us.

Because a number of our players had been to South Africa the year before, we were hounded by demonstrators throughout the tour. In fact, the trouble started as soon as our flight from England landed on the tarmac at Auckland airport.

We transferred to a smaller plane, amusingly called a 'Friendship Flight', for the onward trip to Whangerai and were taxiing down the runway when the control tower radioed the pilot with the warning: 'There could be a bomb on board. Don't take off – and get everyone out.' We abandoned the plane there and then, leaving it stranded in the middle of the runway. It was the last thing we needed after the exhaustions of our flight from London. All we wanted to do was get to our hotel and to bed. Instead, we were left hanging around, bored and weary, as the flight crew waited for the emergency services to give us the all-clear.

The bomb scare predictably turned out to be a hoax but we were in no mood to wait around for steps to be brought out from the terminal building for us to reboard the plane. Being rugby players we decided to go about it our own way. It was quite straightforward really . . . a matter of heaving the first player up, then hoist, shove and pull the others into the aircraft one by one, aided by those already on board. When Andy Simpson's turn arrived, Steve Bainbridge's long arm reached down to heave him up while someone else gave his backside a shunt from below. Unfortunately the double shove carried a little more weight than Andy had bargained for – and his head thudded into the top of the aircraft doorway, to the great amusement of everyone. Apart from poor Andy, that is, because the top of his scalp had been split open by the impact. We then witnessed an equally absorbing sequel which gave a whole new meaning to the expression in-flight entertainment as tour manager Derek Morgan stitched up the wound with the emergency kit he had brought from his dental practice in Newbridge.

That job completed (and for all we knew Derek might have been using a needle and cotton from his wife's sewing box), physio Alan Bell proceeded to swathe the wounded hooker's head in bandages. With his face obliterated and his eyes visible only through tiny slits, he looked like a relic of ancient Egypt and to Andy's increasing embarrassment the boys just cracked up. Talk about adding insult to injury!

That was the first of Alan's *faux pas* – one mile of bandages for a tiny cut! Old Belly, a lovely fella and self-taught physio from the north east collieries, didn't really fill the lads with too much confidence with his diagnoses and treatment. In fact, he must have thought he was on a holiday or had one of the healthiest touring sides ever because private clinics abounded on that tour with players diagnosing and treating each other's injuries.

I was so exhausted that when we arrived at the Settlers Hotel in Whangerai I slept for 14 hours solid. Three days later we took on North Auckland in the first of our two build-up games before facing the All Blacks at Christchurch. It went well for me personally as we coasted home 27–14, then moved on to Gisborne where we thrashed Poverty Bay 45–0. I confidently expected Bainbridge and myself to form the second row partnership in the Tests, and when we were both picked to face Auckland I was convinced this would be the case.

On the strength of the North Auckland game the Kiwi Press wrote off our chances against the All Blacks and dismissed us as unfit and boring; but from the players' point of view it was New Zealand that was boring! Although the country, with its green fields and British traditions, reminded me of home in many ways, everything seemed 25 years behind the times. There was also precious little to do, so it was often a case of making our own entertainment.

In fact, the highlight of the visit as far as the sights were concerned

Who said I'm no angel?

Next stop the South Pole! The 1985 England tour squad at Bluff – 18,912 kilometres from London, and New Zealand's most southerly land-point

'One false move and I'll blow your head off!'

Auckland's Andy Haden and Gary Whetton can only marvel as Steve Bainbridge takes my exquisite pass!

Cock of the North. Picture by Bryan Jackson

World Cup '87 . . . and England's answer to Crocodile Dundee

Bob-a-job (or is it bobby-a-job?) week in Blackpool

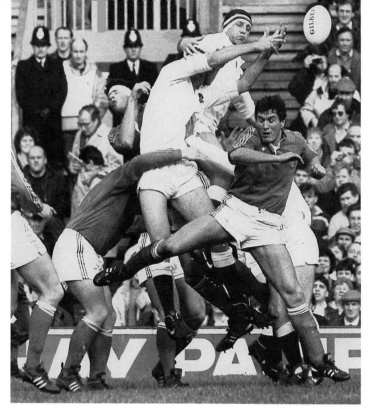

Top of the cops . . . I'm the one without the helmet against France, 1989. Picture by Adam Butler of the Press Association

Stop me if you can . . . Australian captain Nick Farr-Jones is the man trying to in the decisive Third Test at Sydney. Picture by All-Sport/Russell Cheyne

King of the jungle . . . Mike Teague did a great job as Man of the Series for the Lions

You'd think the Lions had won the series!

Mike Teague and I have the last laugh on Australia

The Mean Machine . . . as seen in the Nike advertisement

Pounding the lonely beat at Blackpool. This picture by Mike King of The Observer
captures it all

At home with Sharon, Sophie and baby Sara

would have to be the visit to Bluff – the most southerly point on the New Zealand mainland. Basically there's nothing worth seeing there, just a signpost giving the distances to all the major cities of the world. For those with a geographical leaning, Bluff's latitude is 46 degrees 36 minutes 54 seconds south and longitude 168 degrees 21 minutes 26 seconds east. Or in more simplistic terms, a one-hour coach drive from Invercargill.

The Travel Lodge in Gisborne was pretty typical of New Zealand hotels. During our meal after the match there was a fair bit of banter flying around – as you'd expect after a 45–0 victory. And when Steve Brain started looking for candidates to outdrink him, I joined in the joke by accepting the challenge. Brainer had been dubbed 'cane and coke king' for his alcoholic conquests in South Africa the previous year but in my innocence I thought we'd just knock back a few beers and that would be it.

How mistaken I was! The boys decided a challenge was a challenge and a formal set of rules were laid down, along with a fair few bets. Brainer and I were seated on stools in the middle of the team room and made to nominate our drinks in turn from the table set out alongside us. Beer, cocktails, duty-frees, we swigged down the lot over the next couple of hours. I was just reaching my limit and thinking, 'I'm not long for this world', when through a haze of alcohol I saw Brainer topple off his stool . . . straight on to the drinks table. A great wave of relief came over me as he clattered to the floor, accompanied by a pile of glasses and beer bottles. At that moment, timing his entrance to perfection, in walked England coach Martin Green. He took a quick look at Brainer lying amid the glasses then made a quick U-turn muttering: 'If you're not out there for a full session first thing in the morning, you're on the first plane back to England.'

Poor Brain was in no fit state for anything, let alone taking himself to bed. So, brimming with satisfaction at my great victory, I helped him to his room . . . blissfully unaware of the physical torture that lay ahead.

The following morning the rain was bucketing down and Brainer and I were still feeling much the worse for wear. The squad had a police escort to the training pitch because of the anti-apartheid protestors – and when the session got under way the cops just sat there laughing at the state of the two of us.

Green really put us through it. In fact I swear he had the plane tickets in the back pocket of his tracksuit just waiting for one of us to crack. But we came through it, even if Steve did throw up every time he bent down to touch his toes in the warm-up. And two days later we were both in the team that ran out to face Auckland.

It meant I had played the first three games straight off, which suited me because as long as I was in the side I was fairly confident of keeping my place for the Tests. As I had played well against North Auckland and Poverty Bay – and received good write-ups in the Kiwi Press into the bargain – my case for playing against Auckland had been pretty strong. And although the result didn't go to plan, I played well enough to be sure of keeping my place for the First Test a week later. Or so I thought.

The Auckland second-row combination of captain Andy Haden and the young Gary Whetton was the best I had faced, and that included all of Europe's major national teams. Yet Bainbridge and I did so well in the lineout that veteran All Black Haden praised us in the Press afterwards as the best combination he had played against at Eden Park. That, coming from a man who had been at the top of the world stage for many a year, meant a lot. Unfortunately things hadn't gone quite so well in other departments where Auckland made us look very ordinary. Basically they were just too good for us – very mobile, with a good scrummage, a classy set of backs and a demon kicker in Grant Fox. We lost 24–6 to a side brimming with the cream of New Zealand talent as players like Haden, Fox, the Whetton brothers, Steve McDowell and David Kirk pounded out the message that our fitness just wasn't up to southern hemisphere standards.

I sat out the 25–16 win against Otago the following Wednesday, quietly confident I'd be back for the big one in Christchurch three days later. The performance of Bainbridge and John Orwin as a partnership seemed of little relevance – or the impressive overall display of the team – because I fully expected Bainbridge and myself to be the England pairing against the All Blacks. In fact, it hadn't even crossed my mind that I might lose my Test place for the first time.

As a Liverpool supporter I made a point of getting up at six a.m. on the Wednesday to watch the European Cup final live from Brussels. Instead I watched in disbelief as the Heysel Stadium disaster unfolded. It was to be the first of two stunning blows that day . . .

As I trained with the rest of the boys that morning I had no inkling of what was to follow. When the news came it was brief and to the point. Derek Morgan called me into an ante-room after training and announced curtly that I had been dropped and that Bainbridge and Orwin had been selected in the second row. Just like that. No reason, nothing. Numbed by the shock, and furious that no reason had been given, I managed to pull myself together enough to help the chosen 15 with their training build-up. It was normal practice for the dirt-trackers – the players not in the team – to assist and in any case I had no axe to grind with the other players. My gripe was with Morgan and Green for not giving me a good reason why I had been dropped.

It was eating me up so much that I went back the following day and demanded an explanation. This time Morgan said that I had been benched because the Bainbridge-Orwin pairing was a better scrummaging unit which would be crucial with our largely inexperienced front row of Gary Pearce, Brain and new cap Paul Huntsman. Particularly against an All Blacks front five of Dalton, Knight, Ashworth, Pierce and Gary Whetton.

Still a little confused because my scrummaging had never really been questioned, I looked for a second opinion from coach Green. This only added to the confusion, Martin telling me not to worry. He insisted I hadn't done anything to warrant being dropped – in fact my play had improved ten-fold.

I was up early on the day of the match, still trying to come to terms with the biggest set-back of my career. I went out for a run around the local park on my own, trying to work out just where I had gone wrong and how I was going to get my place back.

By four-thirty that afternoon my tour was as good as over – in my own mind at any rate. The boys had lost the Test 18–13 but scored two tries to none through Mike Harrison and Mike Teague in a performance that exceeded all expectations. The All Blacks are notoriously slow starters when confronting touring sides, and on a filthy day they lived up to their reputation. Inches of rain had fallen in the hours leading up to the game, yet the New Zealand Rugby Union decided in their wisdom to play their customary two or three curtain-raisers prior to the big match. That merely chopped up the Lancaster Oval pitch and added to the treacherous conditions.

We had good reason to be disappointed after losing out to Kieran Crowley's boot, although lack of match practice had been partly responsible for the lacklustre, tryless performance by the Blacks. How different it was going to be in a week's time.

I had a weird mixture of emotions; disappointment at England losing what could have been a famous victory; delight at how well the boys had played; and despair because I knew that barring a sensation I was out of the Second Test as well. During the week between the two

Tests I refused to let my head drop. I was determined to fight to get my place back and although it's not something I'd wish on anyone, there was always the possibility of somebody being injured.

I had one more chance to stake my claim – against Southland at Invercargill on the Tuesday. But although we won 15–9 it was a dour, unsavoury affair that impressed no one. It was a bit like the local delicacy really . . . oysters. I can't stand the sight of them, yet the entire hotel dining-room seemed to revolve around them. It was oysters with everything, the soup, the main course . . . in fact it was a wonder they didn't serve up oyster pudding as well!

The hotel, situated in the centre of what is effectively a one-street town, was like stepping back into the '50s. But Steve Bainbridge and I did at least manage to provide the management and the local Press with a rare bit of excitement by posing for photographs with our legs dangling out of our undersized beds. As my England career progressed I made a point of asking for a double bed wherever we stayed so I could stretch out diagonally. But at that time, being a new boy, I just accepted the situation when I found my 6ft 8in frame condemned to a tiny six-foot single bed – even though I had great difficulty in sleeping.

Predictably I was back on the bench as Bainbridge and Orwin again got the vote for the Wellington Test. My non-selection gave me automatic membership of Bob's Tours, the bitter and twisted club formulated by Bob Hesford and Austin Sheppard to keep the Wednesday side's morale high. It was also Bob's way of making his good-natured point to the management over selection.

The All Blacks had a lot to prove at Athletic Park after their embarrassing experience a week earlier. Stung by some scathing attention from their own Press, they came out in an avenging mood as if to prove a point.

When Jon Hall gave us the lead with a second-minute try it incensed them even more. Steve Brain emerged from the first ruck with the back of his head pouring blood from the attentions of an All Black set of studs and played on with his shirt stained red from a gaping wound that eventually required ten stitches. Then Mike Harrison, or Burglar Bill as he was christened when he scored his second interception try in successive Tests – was flattened by a Mark Shaw punch. It was blatant intimidation and it worked as the Blacks took control and ran in half-a-dozen tries.

We were already 30-odd points down when Orwin limped off with Achilles trouble and I got a run-out for the last quarter of the game.

Within minutes the bad feeling exploded in a massive punch-up involving all 16 forwards.

I settled in quickly to the task in hand, however, and in my short space of time on the park made my mark in the middle of the lineout, taking a number of two-handed catches against Murray Pierce. But there was no way my influence could change the course of the game and we finished on the end of a record 42–15 hiding – England's heaviest defeat of all time. We effectively lost this Test to the New Zealand back row of Murray Mexted, Shaw and Jock Hobbs, who were simply every-where. They were first to the breakdown, driving in low and hard in support of the rest of the pack following behind. And they had obviously worked very hard on driving their lineouts, which bore fruit with a couple of tries. Mexted, for me, was the player of the series with his explosive charges from the base of the scrum.

Our dressing-room afterwards was like a hospital casualty ward with walking wounded being stitched up all over the place. The official count was seven injured – but English pride had also been hurt. We had gone out there believing we were fit, and by northern hemisphere standards we were. But these boys were in a different league and we had an awful lot of catching up to do.

When we got home, suddenly people were asking questions about the structure of English rugby. The county system, divisional champion-ship and Merit Table programme all needed looking at and revamping. English rugby was at its lowest ebb – and above all we had to get ourselves fit.

I counted up the games I had played over the season. With police, Grasshoppers, representatives and England commitments – including the New Zealand tour – it came to 72. Yet All Blacks skipper Andy Dalton, for instance, claimed to play just 18 to 20 times a year, albeit top-class provincial and representative games.

I knew that if I was to stay fresh and survive at the top, I had to cut down drastically on my commitments. It was a policy later to be backed up by Geoff Cooke, who recommended a programme of 30 to 34 matches a season.

The end of this season also saw the demise of Dick Greenwood as England coach. Dick was unable to tour New Zealand but in his short time in the post he'd had problems with several senior players he inherited from predecessor Mike Davis. While the younger members of the squad accepted Dick's ideas without question, hardened inter-nationals like Maurice Colclough, John Scott and John Carleton didn't agree with his coaching methods or the way he ran the side. The upshot of it all was that those players drifted away at a time when they should have been around to help bring on the youngsters in an important period of change.

While Dick had some great ideas, especially on the fitness side, if I was to be critical in any way I would say it was probably his methods of communication that let him down, along with his dealings with senior players.

Sadly, I had had only five matches under Dick's direction. Now it was up to me.

CHAPTER SIX

Cardiff Regrets

MEMORIES of a miserable Wednesday night playing for the Barbarians against Newport sent me into the opening match of the 1986 Five Nations season with some apprehension. David Waters, the lineout man called up by Wales to replace suspended Bob Norster, had given me an uncomfortable time at Rodney Parade and I feared I might have my work cut out against him at Twickenham.

Ironically, he had been selected to play against England at Cardiff 12 months earlier when Norster was injured, only to miss out when the match was postponed and Bob recovered in time for the rearranged fixture. In the event, Waters' long-awaited debut must have been a great disappointment to him because he failed to make any impression at all. Maurice Colclough, who coincidentally had returned from France to play his club rugby in Wales with Swansea, was recalled for his first international in almost two years and his great experience eased the pressure on me to some degree.

I was glad he was on my side this time as he had given me a tough outing earlier in the season when I played against him for the North against London Division at Otley. Since Maurice was an out-and-out four jumper, my England brief was changed to accommodate him. The new policy was for me to move around the lineout in a roving role, alternating between two and four and thereby keep the opposition on their toes. This time there was a complete reversal of the Baa-Baas' defeat at Newport as Maurice and I cleaned out Waters and his partner John Perkins.

Although this was arguably my most impressive England performance so far, the result was in doubt until injury time when Rob Andrew completed a remarkable one-man kicking display with the winning dropped goal. Thanks to his seven kicks we scraped home 21–18, although in career terms that was possibly one of the worst things that could have happened to Rob. Suddenly, on the strength of one match, he was elevated to national hero status. Two days later he appeared as a guest on the Wogan TV show and when we travelled up to Murrayfield for our next game he was on a hiding to nothing.

I had the worst possible build-up to the Scotland clash because I scarcely slept a wink the night before at Peebles Hydro, no thanks to my room-mate Colclough. It was my misfortune to be saddled with the most raucous snorer in the squad, and when Maurice fell asleep before I did there was not the faintest chance of getting any shut-eye. I tried everything from taking sleeping pills to belting him with pillows, with no success whatsoever. In despair I grabbed my blankets, went into the bathroom and spread myself out in the bath. Still the snoring came vibrating through the door so I took the only option left to me. I went down to reception and asked if I could have another room. Getting to sleep at three a.m. was hardly the best preparation for a major international, but that does not explain the disaster that followed the next afternoon.

This was probably the best Scottish combination I was to play against. It had an ideal mix of youth and experience, with the raw talents of the Hastings brothers and Matt Duncan complemented by the vast experience of men like Roy Laidlaw, John Rutherford, Iain 'The Bear' Milne and Colin Deans.

Another drawback from an English point of view was that our team selection was not what it might have been. That became obvious when we lost Jon Hall injured and had no back-row specialist to cover for him. As a result Nigel Redman had the impossible task of coming on as an emergency flanker and trying to counter the daunting Scottish breakaway combination of John Jeffrey, Finlay Calder and John Beattie.

No. 8 Beattie made his intentions clear from the start with a dig from a drop-out which left my right eye virtually shut for the rest of the game. The rampant Scots then proceeded to swarm all over the field and for no apparent reason we fell apart. It was total collapse as we crumbled to a 33–6 defeat, our heaviest ever by Scotland. Gavin Hastings, in only his third international, kicked 21 points while all we could manage in reply to tries by Scott Hastings, Duncan and Rutherford were a couple of Andrew penalties.

Changes were inevitable for the Twickenham clash with Ireland and we took the field on a freezing day with six new caps. One of the new faces was a fellow-policeman by the name of Dean Richards, who was to make such a remarkable impact on England's fortunes over the next few seasons. His arrival not only bolstered the pack, it also brought us our first tries of the season after two blank afternoons. Dean scored two himself from close range while Huw Davies added a third in a 25–20 victory; but the most remarkable thing about the game was that it was played at all. When we went to look at the ground the day before it was like walking on concrete. Yet somehow the ground staff managed with the assistance of tarpaulins and straw to thaw it out sufficiently for the match to go ahead. It was so cold that the players were issued with thermals – which only the backs bothered to wear. And for the only time in my career we actually left the field for a half-time cuppa in the changing-room.

Our season of wildly fluctuating fortunes was completed by the 29–10 drubbing in Paris where I scored my first try for England after taking the ball from a French lineout throw which Jean Condom had deflected over his own line. There was some dispute with hooker Steve Brain as to who scored the try, since we both dived to get the touchdown but in the event I was accredited with the score.

The writing had been on the wall for us early on when at one of the first scrums the French 'popped' our front row of Gareth Chilcott, Brain and Pearce. They went on to score four tries and a penalty try to my lone effort – and the heat of the battle took so much out of Brainer that he collapsed in the dressing-room afterwards.

My disappointment at the Paris result was tempered by my inclusion in the British Lions squad to face the Rest of the World just after the completion of the Five Nations tournament. Flattered as I was, the privilege of facing the world's finest players in that International Board (IB) centenary game was to cost me nearly a year out of international rugby.

The match, played at the Arms Park at the end of April 1986, was the first of two games in four days pitting the best players in the northern hemisphere with the best from Down Under and South Africa.

The four England men in the squad, Brain, Richard Hill, Rory Underwood and myself, were immediately plunged into a ridiculous financial tangle by the pettiness of the RFU. Whilst the other home unions had happily sanctioned daily tour allowances for their players to cover both games, the Twickenham hierarchy decided that since we were not abroad, and the games did not constitute a tour, we were not entitled to a penny. The upshot was that the four of us had to sit and watch as the Scottish, Welsh and Irish players were handed individual envelopes containing their £120 allowance for the week. It was a highly-embarrassing experience, not only for us but also for Rowlands, team coach Mick Doyle and all the other players. Despite pleas from all quarters the RFU refused to budge on their stance, so Clive took it upon himself to see that common sense prevailed. He put his hand in his pocket and made up most of the difference by handing the four of us £90 each from the expenses he had been allocated for incidentals.

The Lions faced such an amazing array of talent in Cardiff that it is worth naming the opposition individually. The Rest of the World took the field on that rainy Wednesday afternoon in April with the following glittering line-up: Serge Blanco, John Kirwan, Andy Slack, Michael Lynagh, Patrick Esteve, Wayne Smith, Nick Farr-Jones, Enrique Rodrigues, Tom Lawton, Gary Knight, Mark Shaw, Steve Cutler, Shalke Burger, Simon Poidevin and Murray Mexted.

The moment that was to shatter my immediate future came some 20 minutes into the game when I took a pass from Rory going up the wing and was tackled from the side by the combined force of Cutler and Rodriguez. An electric shock went through my right knee; it was a horrendous feeling and I knew something was seriously wrong. I came off and when I ran up and down the touchline it felt fine but the moment I started to twist and turn, the knee just gave way.

My injured leg packed in ice, we moved on to London for the second IB celebration game at Twickenham on the Saturday. An orthopaedic surgeon was called to our hotel and he advised me to stay in London so he could operate in Harley Street the following week. He also told me I would be lucky to play again and suggested I considered calling it a day. I could understand his concern since I had torn the medial ligament completely away from the bone. It wasn't as if it was just a stretch, it had completely snapped. But I had no desire to remain in London for surgery and there was no way I was accepting that my rugby career was over.

Before being driven north by a friend from Hoppers I watched the Overseas XV thrash the Five Nations 32–13 at Twickenham and had a real eye-opener regarding the respective qualities of northern and southern hemisphere players. Looking on from the stand rather than playing gave me a totally different perspective, and seeing the likes of Danie Gerber, Roger Gould, Warwick Taylor, Carl de Plessis, Naas Botha, Andy Dalton, Andy Haden, Steve Tuynman and the giant South African prop Flippie Van der Merwe in full cry brought home to me how far behind we were in world terms.

When I arrived home, there was a phone message waiting for me from the Preston orthopaedic surgeon, Chris Faux. Chris, who has strong links with Grasshoppers and is an avid rugby fan, had watched the Cardiff match on television and contacted my wife. Sharon told him what the doctor in London had suspected and an appointment was made for me to go and see Chris the following Monday.

Since I was adamant not to be treated in London as it was so far away from home, I kept the appointment and was operated on the same evening. My right leg was in a full plaster cast for six weeks and I was subsequently off work for four months. My physiotherapist, Patricia Bartley, who specialised in sports injuries and lived in a neighbouring village, started me on a course of intensive treatment whilst still in plaster. When the cast came off, the leg muscles had naturally wasted to half their normal size. Over the next few months, when I was not having treatment from the physio I would spend my every waking hour doing leg-raises with a sandbag to weight my ankle in an attempt to rebuild the muscles. I visited the physio for treatment every day and Patricia worked extremely hard on the leg. It seemed to become her mission in life. A keen long-distance runner and, like Chris, a rugby supporter, she was as determined to see me back on the international field as I was myself. It was thanks to both Chris's skill and Patricia's dedication that I was eventually to make my return to that field.

I was so eager to start playing again that against all medical advice I made myself available for the Divisional Championships the following November. In retrospect I probably rushed myself too quickly. I hobbled through the North's first two divisional games with my knee strapped up and was then dropped by manager Geoff Cooke because I wasn't fully fit. Even though in my own mind I had fully recovered, when I went on England's training week to Portugal in the New Year it was noticeable to everyone except myself that I was still carrying the right leg injury. A combination of a slight limp when I ran and a tendency to jump off the left foot in the lineout was spotted by our new physio Kevin Murphy and fitness adviser Tom McNab, who then went to work with me on redressing the balance and restoring my confidence to use the right leg.

Dave Cusani, the Orrell and Lancashire lock, stepped in to fill the role I had vacated in the North team against London Division; and as a result of his performance in winning what was effectively the Championship final he gained selection alongside Nigel Redman for England's first 1987 Five Nations match against Ireland in Dublin. Having played against Dave at club level on a number of occasions I had always rated him very highly. Although younger than myself he was senior in England terms, having toured South Africa in 1984, and by all accounts was unlucky not to be capped out there. Knowing his pedigree and origins, I felt that if I had to lose my place at least I was losing it to another Lancastrian.

Around that time I left Grasshoppers and joined Fylde. It wasn't that I was unhappy at Preston, far from it in fact. However, it had often been suggested to me that it might be beneficial to my career if I switched to a bigger club. There was gentle persuasion from several sources and I was out of the England team and desperate to get my place back.

Steve Bainbridge and I had discussed the situation and we felt the selectors had us in mind as their second-row pairing now that Steve was available after suspension had ruled him out of the 1985 and 1986 Five Nations campaigns. Although he'd been an England regular in 1983 and 1984 and toured New Zealand with the 1983 Lions, Bainbridge's career had been blighted both by injury and his fiery temperament. The problem was that he was easily wound up and when that happened it was extremely difficult to cool him down. As a result he had been sent off on more than one occasion and the bans which followed had cost him a considerable number of caps.

There were gasps of horror when I told Hoppers I was leaving; and officials were even more stunned to discover I was moving down the road to join our greatest rivals. The two clubs have always been in fierce competition with one another, our annual Boxing Day clash invariably attracting a huge turnout. Since Fylde were traditionally the leading team in the area the news of my move was greeted with strong suspicions within the Preston camp that I had been poached. It simply wasn't true, even though nothing pleased the respective committee men more than putting one over on the rival club. Steve and I had merely mooted the idea and when it got back to Bill Beaumont and the Fylde committee it led to discussions and agreement between them and myself.

I will never know how instrumental the change of club was, but the fact is that when England lost 17–0 in Dublin, Cusani and Redman were axed and the selectors recalled Steve and myself for the next game against France. We lost 19–15 but that was merely a prelude to the Cardiff catastrophe that followed.

I was to stay at Fylde for two seasons. They were a stronger team than Preston at the time, and the first year went well. But I began to miss the old club and kept a foot in both camps by popping in to Hoppers for the occasional beer. During my second season, however, the Fylde side started to break up and Bainbridge decided to move back to his native north-east. By then I had regained my England place so I happily returned to Preston. One thing I did learn from my stay at Fylde was that playing regularly against more highly-rated opposition neither helped nor hindered my ability to make the transition from club to international rugby. The fact is that the step up from junior rugby to England level never presented a problem for me throughout my career. I'm not saying it would work for every international player, but I'm sure that not having to perform in pressure games week in, week out contributed to my continuance in the England team.

After waiting 24 years to beat Wales in Cardiff, England's eagerness to put matters right was verging on desperation. However, when Welsh supporters descended to the level of spitting at us during our pre-match walkabout at the Arms Park it was perhaps inevitable that the rivalry between the two countries would plunge to new depths.

That match was to prove the lowest point of my career, a day on which I was fortunate not to have been asked to take an early bath, and which was to end painfully, both physically and mentally, for many players. It also culminated in the most uncomfortable post-match dinner I have ever attended and ultimately the suspension of myself and three of my team-mates from England's next game.

Cardiff Arms Park has never been my favourite ground; and the vast publicity over the years about our so-called 'jinx' made that elusive victory more important every time we went there. When we strolled out after the Welsh players to inspect the pitch, still wearing our England blazers and slacks, the ground was filling up rapidly. As one might expect we were greeted by a chorus of whistles and jeers from the home supporters, a large number of whom had already gathered on the terracing around the players' tunnel. A blaze of colour awaited us as flag-waving spectators swathed in red and white hung over the sides to get a closer look at the enemy. But while some settled for wafting their flags and scarves in our faces, others decided to take the expression 'within spitting distance' quite literally.

We only became aware of their disgusting behaviour from the mess on our jackets when we reached the safety of the dressing-room area. It was a sickening experience but one which was to be repeated in 1989. Having said that I must emphasise that these were very much isolated incidents. Much as I disliked the hostility I invariably experienced at the Arms Park as a player, I only had to listen to the singing of *Mae Hen*

Wlad Fy Nhadau to understand, even admire, the patriotism of the Welsh. The spitting was inexcusable, however, and merely strengthened our determination to end once and for all the hoodoo that had haunted English sides since 1963.

I was not aware of any particularly bad blood between the teams before the game. Apart from the fact the players did not come face to face until the kick-off, Welsh forwards like Steve Sutton and Phil Davies were old pals and former team-mates of mine in the British Police side. But we had no intention of being intimidated and were absolutely determined to hold our own . . . and to win.

In the changing-room before the game, our volatile skipper Richard Hill was so psyched up he was virtually bouncing off the walls. His feelings were totally understandable. Bath-based players like Hilly, Gareth Chilcott and Graham Dawe were accustomed to winning on Welsh soil at club level, yet for some inexplicable reason the international side had failed in Cardiff time after time. It was not as if the Welsh were unbeatable, just that England always seemed to be psyched-out or incapable of raising their game to the required level. The Welsh were experts at winding the opposition up with their skulduggery. The intimidation was subtle stuff, but in those undisciplined days before Geoff Cooke arrived on the scene, we tended to over-react to the situation. On this occasion the captain's pre-match team talk was lively to say the least. It was a case of lighting the blue touchpaper and standing well back. But we were all 100 per cent behind Richard in our determination to redress the record at the Arms Park. We were sick of England leaving Cardiff with their tails between their legs. It had been a poor Championship showing so far with defeats by both Ireland and France. This was a chance to redeem ourselves, to salvage something from the season and to smash the Cardiff myth.

When the anthems rang out our adrenalin was really flowing; the fervour and passion on the terraces only helped to ignite the fuse. The seeds of the explosion that followed were perhaps sown when Scottish referee Ray Megson, in his first Five Nations game, failed to sort out some early niggling among the forwards. Then, at the second lineout, punches started to fly. Bob Norster aimed an elbow at Steve Bainbridge which missed its target. Instead it smashed into his own teammate Sutton, laying him out with a broken nose. All hell broke out around me but I just followed the play, only to see a Welsh fist flash at Jon Hall as he drove through onto the ball. I saw red, literally. It was a gut reaction, totally spontaneous. I lashed out at Hall's assailant, completely unaware of his identity, and the punch landed with a sickening thud on the side of Davies's face.

Fortunately, from my point of view, Mr Megson and his linesmen had failed to see the blow. Had they done so I think it is a pretty safe bet I would have been asked to leave the field. But although I escaped immediate repercussions, fracturing an opponent's cheekbone with a punch is not something you stand around smiling about, particularly when you realise the victim is someone you regard as a friend. Phil was out of the game and there was nothing I could do about that; it had happened, I had escaped without punishment and now I just had to get on with it.

There was no time to dwell on the matter. The important thing for us, as Richie Collins came on to replace Davies, was to win the game and I had to get my mind back on that goal as quickly as possible. It was rather ironic in the circumstances but the general feeling among the England team was that Collins was a better player than the man he replaced! He went on to emphasise the point by turning in an outstanding performance.

The Cardiff bogey continued as we slumped to a 19–12 defeat and there were to be more serious recriminations over the violence. At one point the media were suggesting I might even face criminal proceedings. As a policeman, the possible consequences of that did not bear thinking about.

I am not trying to excuse my behaviour but the way Davies's injury was subsequently reported in the media made it sound as if his cheekbone had been shattered. As it turned out he had suffered a hairline fracture. The damage, however, had been done and such was the intensity of the feeling that this was one rare occasion when the bad vibes continued after the game and indeed into the post-match dinner at the Angel Hotel. Phil was not there as a result of his injury and I felt bad enough over that. What made me even more uneasy was the attitude, not so much of the Welsh players, but of their wives and girlfriends. Their looks of disgust, along with a number of unsavoury comments aimed in my direction, just added to my discomfort.

Sharon had not made the trip to Cardiff, fortunately as it turned out, and I eventually found solace in an unlikely ally. Steve Sutton had noticed my discomfort and invited me to join him and his wife for a drink in the bar. It was a gesture that I was extremely grateful for and, as we sat in a corner having a quiet beer, as far as we were both concerned the incident was history. It was one of those things that occur in the heat of battle on the rugby field and there was nothing anyone could do about it now.

Nevertheless I had a deep sense of regret over what had happened and also over the fact it had been *allowed* to happen. In my view Mr Megson has to accept a certain amount of blame for not intervening early on when trouble was clearly brewing. I am convinced a stern warning that further offenders would be sent off would have had the desired effect. Instead the bad feeling was allowed to fester and we all know what the upshot of that was. I am not trying to claim I am an angel or to condone my behaviour, but I found it remarkable that it was the English who were branded the villains of the piece, and myself in particular. That feeling became even more intense in the light of subsequent events, when not one Welshman was disciplined or, as far as I am aware, even warned about his conduct.

Although the Welsh players had been just as guilty as we were, the recriminations were all on one side, with my own involvement highlighted on television and throughout the media for several days afterwards. I didn't feel what I had done was significantly worse than some of the other incidents in the game. It just happened to have caused more damage. Yet the media attention my moment of indiscretion attracted was just incredible. The following morning I was pilloried in the Sunday papers, which were already making suggestions about legal action. Then, when I returned to work in Blackpool on the Monday, I learned that three or four camera crews were roaming the town looking for me. There was no way I could do my normal outside job in the circumstances so I spent the day working inside the police station to keep out of the way.

The furore still had not died down the following Wednesday when I was due to play for Lancashire in a Police Athletic Association cup game against Gwent Police at our Hutton headquarters. It was the sort of match that would normally attract maybe 50 or 60 spectators. On this occasion there were hundreds and the majority of them were from the Press and television. They had only come for one reason: to put me under the microscope. It rather incensed me that I should attract all this attention since I had, after all, been just a small cog in a big wheel of violence at Cardiff. If the media people at Hutton were hoping for a repeat of the Arms Park fiasco they must have been bitterly disappointed because the game went off without incident. All this attention was of course a great embarrassment to my superiors in the police and it came as no surprise when I was called in by the Deputy Chief Constable and reprimanded in no uncertain terms. The message was clear; I was a police officer 24 hours a day and was judged not merely by what I did on the streets but also by my actions when I was off duty. What made it worse was that my particular indiscretion had been highlighted on the television news and flashed into half the households in Britain.

The flak was flying from all directions: the media, work and also from Twickenham. When chairman of selectors Mike Weston phoned to say I had been dropped for England's next game as a disciplinary measure it did not come entirely as a surprise. My fellow forwards Chilcott and Dawe were also axed and so was Hill, who as captain on the day was held responsible for our excesses. I had no quibble with the RFU getting tough on the matter and no argument with the decision to drop me. After all, the result of my sins was there for everyone to see. However, Chilcott and Dawe had been no more involved than anyone else in the pack while Hill had had no involvement whatsoever in the violence. It seemed to me he was being made a scapegoat merely because he was the man in charge on the field, or possibly because of his animated pre-match team talk.

The Welsh Rugby Union had been set an example which they should have followed but they chose to do absolutely nothing. It takes two to tango, as the saying goes, and the fact that half the perpetrators escaped with not so much as a warning made our punishment all the more difficult to accept. As it turned out I was lucky in that I bounced straight back the following season. But it proved much more difficult for Chilcott and Hill to re-establish themselves while poor Graham Dawe's England first-team career effectively ended that day.

I was concerned about Phil Davies's condition and there had been much speculation by the Press about the matter being pursued further. So a few days after the game I telephoned his home. Phil's mother answered the call as he was out at the time. From her reaction you would have thought she was talking to a long-lost son. I half-expected her to give me the same cold-shoulder treatment I had received from the Welsh players' wives at the Angel Hotel. Instead I was greeted by a warm-hearted lady who assured me there was nothing to worry about and promised to get Phil to ring me back.

Sure enough he did and the message was simple: forget it. It's over and done with. The sickening aspect from my point of view was that, like myself, he had been hounded by the Press. Local legal representatives were also encouraging him to take further action and offering their services free of charge. It came as a great relief to me that he had told them he wasn't interested.

Whilst the consequences of my next visit to Cardiff were somewhat less dramatic, the 1989 match against Wales was every bit as traumatic. The England success story had by now begun and although the Scots had drawn at Twickenham, we were clear favourites to record a victory at the Arms Park which would have given us the Championship outright with seven points out of eight.

Once again the hostility was in evidence; so was the spitting and the anti-English feeling. It was destined to be another afternoon of niggling nastiness and in terrible conditions the Welsh took literally seconds to make their intentions clear. Straight from the kick-off Mike Teague was taken out by a shoulder charge and left the field so concussed that for the next 24 hours he hardly knew where he was.

That blow could well have cost us the match since it took away one of my chief lineout support players; and the game subsequently turned into a disaster for Paul Ackford and myself. Bob Norster had another stormer against me in the middle, while Phil Davies's brief at the front was to wipe Ackers out at every lineout. With a southern hemisphere referee, Kerry Fitzgerald, who let everything go, we never got a sniff of any decent lineout ball.

Welsh scrum-half Robert Jones did exactly the right thing in such filthy conditions, kicking everything from the base of the scrum to keep the pressure on us. He constantly put the ball in the air, and with Jonathan Webb repeatedly clattered as it came down we seemed to be perpetually pinned in our half. Yet we might still have won but for a Welsh try that never was. Rory Underwood popped a loose pass inside which Webb mishandled; and when the Welsh players charged through, Mike Hall made a despairing but unsuccessful dive at the ball. It seemed clear he had not scored but it summed up our luck that Fitzgerald awarded the try despite being unsighted, and Wales went on to win 12–9. Once again England had failed to live up to all expectations.

It also summed up my personal jinx at Cardiff, the one place I had never won a game at any level, be it for England, the Lions, the Barbarians or even the British Police. The sequence even incorporated the one England game I *watched* at the Arms Park, when Bill Beaumont's boys were 'conned' out of victory by a last-minute penalty in 1981. The only good thing about that game was that I actually got in for nothing . . . courtesy of the South Wales Constabulary. The Lancashire Police team were on tour at the time but since we had no tickets for the big game we were all temporarily assigned to the local force – as the Cardiff Pickpocket Squad! The gatemen were left totally bemused as 30 scruffy lads in jeans and sweatshirts were escorted by uniformed police into the stadium and on to the Westgate Street terrace.

We were already celebrating an historic win when, with England clinging to a flimsy 19–18 lead, scrum-half Brynmor Williams dummied to pass from a scrum in one final despairing effort to pull the game round for Wales. Centre Clive Woodward strayed inches offside in front of the posts and up stepped Steve Fenwick to kick the winning penalty and ruin the day for us.

Whilst my police colleagues and I found that experience disappointing, it was nothing like as painful as the embarrassing British Police game played on the adjoining Cardiff Rugby Club pitch some time afterwards. We were thrashed 62–0 by a New Zealand Combined Services side which was actually a combination of the Armed Services and the NZ police; and with Wayne Shelford and several top Maoris in their ranks they were quite some team. Certainly they had wiped out all opposition in this country, so it had been somewhat reluctantly that I drove down to the Welsh capital on the day of the match accompanied by my Lancashire team-mates and Merseyside policemen, Nigel Heslop and Sean Gallagher.

As luck would have it, the British team that took the field bore no resemblance to the one that had been published. Apart from the absence of Dean Richards and other top police players, Heslop and Gallagher found themselves dropped because we had failed to turn up for the previous day's training session. Unable to explain the idiosyncrasies of the selectors, I was left bewildered when they were relegated to the bench while my 'punishment' was to be appointed captain! In place of Nigel and Sean we had policemen drawn literally off the streets of Cardiff to face Shelford and his Kiwi marauders; players who were basically just second and third team calibre. It was no contest and I proceeded to compound the problem with what must rank as one of the most counter-productive half-time team talks on record. We were 20–odd points behind when I called the lads around me and, voicing prejudices drawn from my Cardiff rugby experiences, demanded: 'Come on, let's show these Welsh ******s in the stands just what we can do.'

Gallagher overheard my verbals as he brought on the half-time oranges and cringed as he made a quick bee-line back to the bench. He still delights at taking off that moment of madness when I forgot that 12 of our 15 players were Welshmen. When Sean explained the significance of the statement to me afterwards, if there was ever a time when I wished the ground would open up and swallow me, that was it.

As a spectator, player and even captain my Cardiff misery seemed
to know no bounds – and there was even an element of bitterness when
I finally tasted victory at the Arms Park exactly ten years after my ill-
fated visit to watch Bill Beaumont's team. England's Welsh hoodoo
finally ended in January 1991, 14 games and almost 28 years to the day
since Richard Sharp had led his side to a 13–6 win on a bitingly-cold
winter's afternoon. Considering the significance of the occasion, one
might have expected Will Carling to lead us on a lap of honour with
players thumping the air in delight and gallons of champagne knocked
back in the changing-room. Instead my one and only taste of success in
Wales came as a bit of an anti-climax.

Our victory was to be the springboard for the Grand Slam glory
that had just eluded us in that winner-take-all Murrayfield finale the
previous season. But it was a remarkably low-key affair, soured by a
players' stand against the RFU which ultimately proved counter-productive. Because of Twickenham's intransigence over what players could
and couldn't do off the pitch, our representatives took it upon themselves
to approach the BBC and ask for £5,000 for after-match interviews. That
was refused . . . and when the BBC complained to the RFU it blew up
out of all proportion.

We felt one way of making our point to Twickenham was to cut
out the customary after-match interviews with both the TV and Press.
Unfortunately it backfired because the media built the 'snub' into their
biggest story of the season and took all the emphasis away from our
achievement on the field. Whilst Geoff Cooke was reportedly embroiled
in the affair, I honestly believe his prime motivation was to keep the
players away from media hype in order to prevent over-confidence for
the games ahead. The memories of our failure at the last hurdle in both
1989 and 1990 were still all too fresh in everyone's mind.

The atmosphere in Cardiff before the game was entirely different
to my earlier experiences. The arrogance of the Welsh supporters had
gone; in fact, despite their remarkable record against us over almost three
decades they seemed resigned to defeat. Wales were deep in the doldrums
and since we had beaten them by a record score at Twickenham the
previous year anything but an England victory would have been a major
sensation. However, we had gone to Cardiff before as hot favourites to
beat poor Welsh sides . . . and lost. So there was no way the team
management were going to allow us to forget it.

Geoff had already decided to change our previous routine of staying
out of town until the day of the game by moving us from our Gloucester

base to a Cardiff city-centre hotel two days before the game. RFU technical administrator Don Rutherford had also prepared a special audio tape to remind us of the job in hand – a compilation of Welsh music featuring a choral rendition of their national anthem. Anyone inclined to doze off got a rude awakening with the strains of *Land of My Fathers* blaring out over and over as our double-decker team bus headed across the Severn Bridge and along the M4 towards the Welsh capital.

In Cardiff itself, we were no longer peppered with the jibes that had spiced up our previous confrontations with Wales. The edge had gone and when Paul Ackford and myself took a walk past the castle and through the main shopping precinct on the morning of the game we were amazed how quiet it was. There were plenty of supporters about but they all seemed to be English. The few Welsh fans we came across were very quiet and tame; it appeared they knew the writing was on the wall. Yet we still had to overcome the psychological barrier of not having triumphed at the Arms Park for 28 years. For a player like myself who had *never* won any form of game at Cardiff it remained a big hurdle to surmount.

We concentrated on keeping the game tight (and were subsequently criticised for it), pounding away up front and using the driving play of Mike Teague as a potent weapon. It was not pretty but it was effective and Mike had sweet revenge for his 1989 nightmare when he scored the game's only try, Simon Hodgkinson's boot doing the rest in a 25–6 victory.

We had done it at last . . . yet somehow the sense of occasion was all a bit deflated. In fact, back in the changing-room it was completely flat because there wasn't a champagne cork popping anywhere. We had laid the bogey to rest once and for all yet the general consensus among the players was 'What's all the fuss about?'. For years before, a result like that would have been the highlight of England's year, yet now it had happened it was merely another victory in a sequence of wins leading hopefully to a Grand Slam. It showed how times and attitudes had changed.

CHAPTER SEVEN

Disaster Down Under

IF I could get any consolation from the previous season's events and the 1987 Cardiff fiasco, it was that chairman of selectors Mike Weston made it clear I was still in contention for the England squad to travel to Australia for the inaugural World Cup a couple of months later. While it choked me that I was forced to miss a cap when I was eager to play, I suppose it could have been worse since in my enforced absence the boys avenged our thrashing by the Scots the previous year by recording an impressive 21–12 Calcutta Cup victory at Twickenham. Nigel Redman and Steve Bainbridge did well together in the second row, but any fears that I might not be recalled for the World Cup were quickly dispelled when all four Arms Park 'villains' were recalled for the trek Down Under to the World Cup.

It was my second long-haul trip after New Zealand in 1985, and very much a journey into the unknown for everyone concerned. With 16 competing nations spread between Australia and New Zealand, it was inevitable that an embryo tournament of such magnitude would be beset by teething troubles. To start with, the decision to stage the event in two different countries was doomed from the outset. The logistics were all wrong and throughout the tournament it seemed to the eight Australian-based teams that there was a totally different competition taking place amongst the eight teams based on the other side of the Tasman Sea.

The inaugural dinner we attended at the Mayfair Crest Hotel in Brisbane was timed to coincide with a simultaneous event across the water, but in retrospect the whole tournament could and should have been played in New Zealand. With the facilities there and a rugby-crazy public, big crowds would have been guaranteed at virtually every game. Apart from the geographical problems entailed in staging such a big tournament in countries 1,500 miles apart, the Australian public showed a distinct lack of interest during the early stages. In almost any other country, a curtain-raiser between the host country and their oldest rivals would surely attract a capacity crowd. For the fickle Aussie fans, however, even the appetising thought of putting one over the Poms failed to lift the lethargy.

The administrators also boobed by playing the game at the Concord Oval, a purpose-built brand-new stadium way outside Sydney. Why the New South Wales Rugby Union had built it nobody seemed quite sure. It took us a good 45 minutes to reach the ground from our hotel and the consensus of Aussie opinion was that the Sydney Cricket Ground (SCG) would have been a far more suitable setting. Not only was the SCG right in the centre of the city, it was also a traditional rugby venue with a 52,000 capacity as opposed to less than 20,000 who turned up at the Concord Oval. The Aussie rugby authorities have obviously taken note of public opinion and attendances there in recent years, because international matches have since been moved to the 40,000-seater Sydney Football Stadium, which stands in the shadow of the SCG.

The Aussies duly fulfilled their status as Pool One favourites by winning 19–6, aided by a David Campese try that never was. We were level 6–6, thanks to a try by skipper Mike Harrison, when the ball was knocked out of Campo's hand after he chased a chip through from Michael Lynagh. He has since admitted that he never grounded the ball but Kiwi referee Keith Lawrence thought otherwise so four points went down the pan for us. Lynagh finished up with 11 points from three penalties and a conversion, and with Simon Poidevin scoring a second try it was not the most auspicious start to our campaign. For fullback Marcus Rose the trauma was compounded since his tour ended there and then when he was badly concussed tackling Peter Grigg. He had to be flown home . . . and we never saw him in the England camp again.

The important thing now was to dispose of Japan and the United States to assure ourselves of finishing runners-up and meeting either Wales or Ireland in Brisbane in the quarter-final. It didn't bother me at the time that I missed out on the Japan game, since team juggling was part and parcel of the World Cup squad system.

However, Japan remains one of the few recognised rugby nations I have never played against, or even visited. Because of my knee injury, I missed England's clash with them at Twickenham the previous autumn, and although I had several offers to play over there during my career, I was unable to accept any of them. In retrospect, perhaps it's just as well – because judging from the average Japanese's lack of inches I'd be quite a novelty walking through Tokyo! They certainly had no answer to our extra size and power in that qualifying game and our ten-try, 60–7 romp remains England's record score in a Test match.

For all that the Japanese have surprised sides over the years, overcoming their lack of inches with ingenuity, commitment and a feel for the game. Worldbeaters they may never be, but a colourful and worthwhile ingredient to world rugby they certainly are. The grand old gentleman of the Japanese RFU, chairman Shiggy Konno, summed up their problems by highlighting the unfairness of racial characteristics which dictate that whenever they discover a 6ft 3in 'giant' the western world invariably responds with a new breed of 6ft 8in locks. Perhaps the answer for Shiggy lies in the debatable tactic the Scots and Irish have developed in recent years of 'adopting' players with tenuous national qualifications. Between the two sides they seem to have fielded as many English-born players over the past couple of seasons as we have . . . not to mention the odd New Zealander or Aussie thrown in for good measure.

I had the pleasure of scoring my second Test try in the 34–6 victory over the USA. We already had the game won when I picked up a bobbling ball a few yards out and drove over the Eagles' line. Now the scene was set for a quarter-final showdown with the Welsh in Brisbane, just three months after that vitriolic affair in Cardiff. We knew when the tournament started that it was on the cards and in the circumstances would have preferred to have faced the Irish. But it wasn't to be and no sooner had the draw been confirmed than the media started predicting another war. The England management promptly swallowed it – and decided to play me out of position to avoid a potential flashpoint with Bob Norster. Mike Weston and coach Martin Green never admitted as much, but that can be the only logical reason for their decision to switch me to the front of the lineout, a position that was totally alien to me, and give Nigel Redman the task of dealing with my arch-rival, Norster.

One of the all-time better decisions by the England management and RFU committee was the selection of the location for the squad four-day R and R break between the pool matches and the quarter-final. In all the years of touring I have visited some fairly exotic locations – Fiji, Bermuda and Hong Kong to name but a few. Hamilton Island stands on its own. Part of the Whitsunday Islands just off the Queensland Coast, it was out of this world – a dreamy little paradise island of palm trees, tropical sun, clear blue seas and golden beaches. My abiding memory of the place is tucking into my bacon and eggs breakfast next to the dolphin pool overlooking Cat's Eye Beach and the bay beyond. The windows of the restaurant opened out on to the pool, and the dolphin, old Flipper, spent the morning bringing his ball to the window, resting his chin on the window sill and waiting for it to be winged across the pool for him to fetch. It was like having to entertain the dog whilst sitting at the breakfast table . . . and the constant interruptions certainly didn't do much for the digestion!

This was the first of several trips to the Barrier Reef. We were also flown 40 miles out to sea by helicopter and landed on a helipad floating above the coral. From there we were able to investigate the underwater delights using snorkels and a glass-bottomed boat, our guide assuring us that sharks never came over the reef and we were quite safe. Nevertheless I kept one eye on the horizon and once or twice did a pretty good impersonation of Mark Spitz as I sprinted back to the pontoon after spotting an imaginary fin on the surface of the water.

Coach Martin Green, blissfully unaware of the tide fluctuations that affect the reef, had good reason to remember the outing. In his eagerness to get into the sea he stripped off and dived into what he believed to be several feet of water . . . only to scrape his entire body across the live coral. Martin was not the happiest of people at the best of times and his straight-faced pallor reminded me of an out-of-work undertaker. His sense of humour was so non-existent that when Steve Brain snipped the crotch out of his underpants and the toes off his socks during a training session in Australia he pretended nothing had happened. On this occasion, however, the poor guy's misery was understandable. He looked as if someone had slashed his face and body with a razor, and because of the danger of infection he spent the next few days striped in iodine – much to the amusement of the players.

There was more hell in store for Martin at Ballymore, and indeed for all of us. We went into the Wales game full of confidence, the memory of Cardiff pushed right to the back of our minds. All that mattered was beating the Welsh and qualifying for the semi-final . . . yet for some unaccountable reason we chose that day to turn in one of England's most ineffective Test performances ever. Not only did we let ourselves down, we also let down millions of fans back home who got up in the small hours to watch the disaster on television.

It did not help that I was pitted against Welsh skipper Richard Moriarty at the front of the line in a role I had virtually no experience of. I found it difficult to acclimatise and as a result our lineout threat was nullified while we simply did not perform in any phase of the game.

Welsh scrum-half Robert Jones continually pinned us back with his sniping box kicks, as he has done so many times over the years, and we had no answer. The crunch came when prop Paul Rendall had to go off with a serious eye injury and while we were waiting for Gareth Chilcott to replace him the Welsh took advantage of the disruption and shunted us back towards our own line to score a try.

Although they won 16–3, Wales also had precious little to boast about after being party to probably the worst international match I have ever played in. It was a dismal day, a dismal game . . . and a dismal end to England's first World Cup. It was bad enough having been heavily beaten in New Zealand in 1985, slaughtered by the Scots in '86 and hammered by the French just a few months previously. This time, however, we had not only been beaten, we had been an embarrassment . . . and the stakes could not have been higher.

The bottom had dropped out of our world and if there had been a plane leaving Brisbane for England that night, we'd have been on it like a flash. As it was we had to settle for drowning our sorrows in Aussie lager and waiting until the following day to return home with our tails between our legs. All that mattered was getting as far away as we could from the scene of the disaster – and as quickly as possible. Things had to change. Quite apart from the embarrassment of the whole affair and being involved in the worst game of the entire World Cup, it left a sickening feeling in the pit of the stomach – and one that made early retirement seem very tempting. We lost a good deal of self-respect that day.

The nightmare heralded the end for Weston and Green as England's management team. In a weird way our failure in Australia was also a blessing in disguise, because it signalled a major turning point in English rugby attitudes. A few months later, in November 1987, Geoff Cooke was brought in as team manager, and he immediately pointed out that our fitness levels were just not good enough – certainly in comparison with the southern hemisphere giants. That message was to be pounded home to us again the following summer when we toured Australia. But if one man was responsible for the renaissance of the team and the glorious successes that were to follow over the next few years, it was Geoff.

I already knew the quiet Yorkshireman from his involvement as manager of the North side that had won the Divisional Championship the previous season. It was he who had phoned me when I was dropped for the final game of that tournament because I had been carrying my

knee injury in the two earlier games. That decision was a big disappointment for me since we had won both matches and were on the point of
winning the title.

The North had quite a team in those days prior to the departure of
players like Will Carling, Rob Andrew and Peter Winterbottom to
London. But while Geoff's decision to give my place to Dave Cusani
was painful, it finally brought home to me a fact I had not until then
been prepared to accept. I had been so desperate to return to playing,
whatever the cost, that it was plain to everyone but myself that I was
not 100 per cent fit. Basically I had been jumping off one leg, and in fact
I was to spend the rest of that season building myself back to full fitness.

At that time, Geoff was still a relative stranger to me. He was never
a man of many words but would really come into his own at pre-match
team talks, in-putting ideas and pointing us in the direction he wanted
us to take. And if anyone overstepped the mark, he could also be a pretty
mean customer.

Before Geoff's arrival in the England set-up, it had been acceptable
practice for the boys to have a few beers in the build-up to an
international. That was kicked straight into touch as he immediately
imposed a strict 'no alcohol after Wednesday' rule. The new discipline
was to rub off so effectively that these days the majority of the England
players don't touch a drop for a full week before a game.

We were also eating all the wrong foods. For instance, it was
considered quite normal under the old regime to dine on steak on the
Friday evening before a game, despite the advice of dieticians that red
meat of that type took something like 24 hours to work its way through
the system. Under Geoff, we were gradually weaned off our old eating
habits and introduced to a pre-match diet of sensible energy foods like
pasta, carbohydrates and easily digested foods like fish and chicken. A
team of fitness advisers was also brought in headed by Scotsman Tom
McNab, a top athletics coach, and at first the players couldn't fathom
out the logic of some of his ideas. Tom brought in training drills which
became part of our squad session warm-up, and he would also work on
specialist aspects like posture and speed of step when running. He also
introduced a running drill called 'jelly jaw' which involved players
sprinting, head perfectly still, keeping the jaw as loose as possible. The
boys often joked that if you ran like that in a match and someone hit you
from the side you'd have no jaw at all, let alone a jelly jaw!

Despite our initial reservations about the value of Tom's tech-
niques, and the good-natured ribbing perpetually aimed in his direction,

we all grew fond of the old Jock and gradually he won the respect of the players. He was a keen rugby follower, having played the game himself at junior and veteran level, and although England use his running drills a lot less these days, I benefited considerably from them and from his fitness schedules recommending distances I should be running and the length of rest periods.

Tom also introduced extensive fitness testing, headed by the dreaded bleep test as we called it. I'll come on to the bleep test in a moment, but he would regularly put the squad through a sequence of disciplines to check our overall fitness, including 30 and 60 metre sprints, sit-ups, press-ups, standing jumps and a strength test. Then there were tests for body-fat content which became more and more challenging as our percentages were reduced. In the first year under Tom, the acceptable level was set at 15 per cent. With one or two exceptions, the forwards started well above that figure – and indeed so did some of the backs. My initial test showed a body-fat level of 19 per cent, but that was nothing compared to some of the boys. Gareth Chilcott, for example, registered so high that I'm sure he went right off the scale. And he was not on his own as a number of players got the infamous black spot for excess body fat. At the opposite end, fliers like Rory Underwood and Chris Oti, who hadn't an ounce of fat on them, came out with ridiculous figures like six per cent. They were percentages no forward, however fit, could ever expect to match – only envy.

Clearly most of us had to start streamlining our bodies by shedding the excess fat and replacing it with muscle. The body-fat tests were all conducted together, with an incentive to record a lower percentage than the next man . . . and utilise any little trick to cut corners. Paul Rendall cottoned on to the idea that if you didn't drink anything for three days before the test, your body fat would be considerably reduced. How he worked that one out I don't know but it was an example of the eagerness of players to gain any possible advantage. He would drag himself to the testing weekend totally dehydrated but in his own mind markedly slimmer.

Levels would fluctuate each time tests were carried out, but the lowest reading I ever recorded was just over 11 per cent. That was quite a contrast with someone like Paul Ackford, who for some reason could never get his body fat appreciably below that crucial 15 per cent. He was exceptionally fit and worked just as hard as everyone else in the squad, if not harder. Yet he always seemed to carry a higher percentage of fat than anyone else and the lowest he ever got down to was something like 14.7 per cent. Try as he might, Paul's body-fat content was invariably higher than a lot of the forwards. I got a lot of satisfaction out of this and it compensated for his claim that he could measure my sprint times with a sundial!

The bleep test, or VO2 Max test to give it its official title, was the one that really got the boys on edge. We would be tested three or four times a year by Rex Hazeldine and his team of fitness experts from Loughborough University, and were expected to show improved results from the previous test. It was such a nightmarish experience that no one would eat breakfast beforehand and you could feel the tension among the players. The test probably lasted about 15 minutes, but to me it seemed to go on for hours. Basically, it entailed running over a 20-metre course at gradually increasing pace levels dictated by a tape machine – until you collapsed with exhaustion. There were 20 or more levels, but by level 11 or 12 some of the boys would invariably start to fall by the wayside . . . and no one survived beyond 16 or 17. There was no hiding place either because if your fitness level hadn't improved since the previous test, questions would be asked.

We began the 1988 Five Nations Championship with a new management team of Geoff in charge with Roger Uttley as coach – the partnership that over the next four years was to steer England to our best sequence of Five Nations results for more than half a century. Geoff set about producing a settled squad, rather than the perpetually-changing hotch-potch of players that had epitomised the set-up during my early years in the side. Yet for the next 12 months, our results – on paper at least – remained as inconsistent as ever.

We weren't expected to win our opening game in Paris but we very nearly did. Ultimately, we lost 10–9 because of a mistake by skipper Mike Harrison, whose fumble let Laurent Rodriguez in for a try he should never have had. Yet up front we played exceptionally well and took their forwards apart in what was probably the start of the rot for France because we have never lost there since.

That game also marked the debut of a young centre who was to make a huge impact on England's future fortunes – Will Carling. He was just 22 and still at Durham University, yet he immediately struck me as an extremely confident young man. But no one, with the possible exception of Geoff Cooke, could have predicted that within a few months he would be captaining the side.

When Wales beat us 11–3 at Twickenham, visions of the wooden spoon were looming large. But the tide began to turn at Murrayfield, where we avenged that horrendous thrashing two years earlier by keeping it tight in a drab game and grinding our way to a 9–6 win. Naturally the Scots started complaining that we had ruined the game with our tactics . . . but the main thing was that we got what we went there for.

That day is remembered more for what happened *after* the match with the Calcutta Cup ending the evening as much the worse for wear as the players! By the time the historic trophy was damaged, I was spark out in my room after a night of mayhem which began perfectly reasonably with a few beers to celebrate England's first victory on Scottish soil since 1980 – not to mention sweet revenge for our hammering two years previously.

The real action began when we arrived for our dinner at the Carlton Highland Hotel to find the rival forwards were all seated together on long tables liberally decorated with full bottles of Scotch. The Calcutta Cup was on display and with the Scots playing perfect hosts, we were soon knocking the whisky back. As our spirits soared so the proceedings began to disintegrate into sheer chaos. Next target was the red-hot dinner plates. The Scots were aware that a hot plate shatters if you tap it in the centre with a spoon, and suddenly we all found ourselves sitting with broken plates in front of us!

The whisky was flowing freely all the time and the last thing I remember is someone passing an over-sized leather football to me for autographing. It was huge, more like a medicine ball. I signed and passed it on somewhat energetically over my head, only to see it land smack in the middle of the committee table behind – much to the disgust of one geriatric Scottish committee man. Across the table from me, Damian Cronin was sitting with his face in his dinner and as I was myself beginning to feel rather grotty, I decided it was time I disappeared.

My wife Sharon, who had been at the ladies' dinner, came looking for me not long afterwards and found me collapsed in my room . . . spark out to the world. The following morning, I got up with a thick head and the full extent of the excesses began to surface. It appeared that the Calcutta Cup had gone missing from the hotel – and been taken for a walk half-way around Edinburgh by Dean Richards and John Jeffrey. The joke among the boys was that it finished up so flattened that it was renamed the Calcutta Plate! During the revelry, a former Blackpool police superintendent in Edinburgh for the match was given a personal insight into the festivities as he descended the stairs at one of the nearby hotels. Suddenly the main door of the hotel swung open and in whistled the Calcutta Cup . . . with Richards and Jeffrey following rapidly behind in a somewhat dishevelled state.

The wide publicity the incident received led to both players being disciplined, and that in itself created some bad feeling between the respective Unions because Jeffrey received a stiffer punishment than Richards. Both players were suspended, but while Dean was forced to miss just the Millennium international against Ireland, the Scots ruled JJ out of an entire tour.

As far as the boys were concerned, it had all been a bit of a giggle, irresponsible maybe but typical of the sort of high jinks that have always gone on in rugby. People had had a few drinks too many, and it had got out of hand. At the end of the day, however, an important rugby heirloom had been damaged and some action had to be taken against the perpetrators. The stumbling block was the inconsistency of the punishment and we felt that the one-game ban Dean got was probably just about right.

The upshot of that incident was that nowadays players tend to be split up with committee men at dinners to avoid the risk of excessive revelry, while security officers are now assigned to protect the Calcutta Cup. In fact, there may well have been security men on duty at the Carlton Highland that night . . . only they didn't fancy tackling Dean and JJ!

After our Murrayfield win, we set ourselves up nicely for the Australian tour with a handsome six-try win over Ireland at Twickenham, then completed a unique double by beating them in a special Test at Lansdowne Road to celebrate the Dublin Millennium.

That game was a special thank-you from the Irish for not deserting them in the early 1970s when the political troubles were at their worst and the other home nations refused to visit Dublin. It was also an occasion when one of Micky Skinner's practical jokes rebounded on him rather painfully. His party piece is usually reserved for men . . . be they waiters, players or whatever. Skins will ask innocuously: 'How do you call a taxi in Paris?' Then, as the unsuspecting victim follows his gaze towards the ceiling, Micky tweaks the poor guy's most private possessions with his hand. Depending on the degree of tweaking and amount of offence taken, the target either crumples up laughing or storms off in disgust. Diplomacy is not, however, one of Skins' strongest points and at this particular function things went badly wrong. Accidentally or not, his Micky-taking backfired and he ended up tweaking the lady-friend of Irish flanker Phil Matthews. Needless to say the tweaking went down like a lead balloon and the punchline came at the first lineout in that Millennium game when Matthews put Micky's nose out of joint – literally. Poor Skins played the rest of the game with a broken nose but he did get the message. He knew he'd overstepped the mark, and Matthews had settled a matter of honour in time-worn fashion. That was the end of it as far as they both were concerned . . . but Micky doesn't try the old party piece on too many ladies these days!

We returned to Australia that May, somewhat apprehensive after our World Cup experiences the previous year, with a taxing programme of nine games in four weeks including three Tests – two against the Wallabies and one in Fiji.

Mike Harrison had given way to Nigel Melville as skipper earlier in the year. But then Nigel suffered a serious knee injury against Ireland in what was to prove his final international and by the time we toured, John Orwin had become our third captain of 1988. On the management side Geoff Cooke, in the absence of Roger Uttley, was assisted by Alan Davies (later to take charge of Wales) and North of England coach Dave Robinson. It was a comparatively inexperienced squad, so much so that after Gary Pearce and Rory Underwood I was the third most-capped player with 21 appearances. There was a lot of young blood in the party as Geoff concentrated on building for the future, and establishing the settled squad that had been so lacking up to that point.

The tour got off to a spectacular start at our preliminary training camp at the North Queensland resort of Kohuna Beach, another exotic sub-tropical location in the style of Hamilton Island. After the blustery spring weather in England, the scorching sun, sea and palm trees were sheer paradise. I sat out our first game, a 39–7 romp against a Queensland Country XV, but that was merely a warm-up for the more testing schedule ahead.

The match against the Queensland senior side five days later provided a much more meaningful indication of how we would fare in the Tests. It was expected to be one of the toughest matches of the tour, and so it proved. We managed to win 22–18, thanks largely to a solid pack performance, and followed that up by beating Queensland B 19–7 in Toowoomba. With three victories under our belts we went into the first Test at Ballymore with high hopes of avenging our World Cup defeat at Concord Oval. The fact that England had lost all four previous Tests against the Wallabies in Australia provided an extra incentive for victory. We were the only International Board country never to have beaten them on their own territory but our respective records at the time suggested we had an excellent chance of putting that record straight. Australia had lost four and drawn one of their previous five Tests while we arrived in Brisbane on the back of three straight victories – one against Scotland and two against the Irish. Yet for some reason we still went into that opening Test with the tag of underdogs.

Like us, Australia were in the process of rebuilding, with a new captain in Nick Farr-Jones and Bob Dwyer having taken over from Alan Jones as coach. They could not have made a worse start because inside the first 20 minutes they gifted Rory Underwood and John Bentley interception tries and suddenly found themselves 13–3 adrift. That lead would have been even greater had Rory not been caught from behind by Ian Williams as he looked for non-existent support after breaking clear. We then proceeded to shoot ourselves in the foot by conceding no fewer than 16 penalties and with Michael Lynagh kicking six of them, somehow managed to lose the game 22–16. Whilst the backs shone, up front we had a torrid time at both the scrum and lineout, losing out to the bigger Aussie eight.

We still hadn't learnt to win – and the factors that had let us down were fitness and discipline, the two priorities in Geoff Cooke's programme for success. We had let a commanding lead slip away through indiscipline and failure to keep the pressure on the Aussies at crucial times. It was reminiscent of our experience in New Zealand in 1985, when we outscored the All Blacks 2–0 on tries in the first Test, yet still lost to Grant Fox's six kicks. And it emphasised once more the need to control ourselves on the park and not give stupid penalties away.

We got little consolation from the news that across the water New Zealand had thrashed luckless Wales 52–3 and 54–9 in what must rank as one of the most ill-conceived tours of all time. What we now had to do was pick ourselves up and try to level the series by winning the second Test in Sydney two weeks hence. We didn't have much to smile about that weekend . . . but we did have a laugh in Adelaide three days later when we played South Australia in a match that left my second-row partner Nigel Redman flushed with embarrassment!

We were all psyched-up when the referee knocked on the dressing-room door and the two teams headed into the tunnel. Out went the Aussie boys on to the pitch and we were about to head for the opposite end when someone noticed Ollie was missing. We didn't need a search party because everyone knew where he was. As any Bath player will tell you, Ollie had a tendency to go to the loo just before a game – not just a bladder job, either. Of course, he can't go half-an-hour before the game like anyone else; it's got to be the last thing he does when everyone else is firing on all cylinders and raring to go. As luck would have it the national anthem struck up prematurely as we waited for Redman. There we were singing away . . . 15 men on the pitch, the English 14 in the tunnel and one sitting it out in the bowels of the changing-room. Needless to say, RFU president John Burgess was not too pleased with the lack of etiquette!

Back on the training park some of Dave Robinson's coaching methods didn't go down too well with the forwards. A true northerner of farming stock, he brought a shepherd's crook with him which he would hold up in training, giving the optimum height for the forwards to bend and run under prior to driving into tackle bags. Anybody who failed the test got a reminder with the crook across the back but there was no way we were having that. So when Dave gave the order, the boys gave it the charge . . . and to this day he doesn't know which of us snapped his prized possession, rendering it useless.

Our morale took another blow when we lost 23–12 to New South Wales in a game which ended with Gareth Chilcott and their prop Peter Kay scrapping in the mud after the final whistle and having to be separated by the other players.

I didn't play in that one because of injury, but when Cooch tried to shake Kay's hand at the end, the Aussie took a swing at him instead. Cooch predictably responded in kind – and the two of them ended up rolling around on the deck. Apparently Kay took exception to an incident in which he reckoned Chilcott had stamped on him. Whether he did or not I don't know, but once the final whistle goes that should be the end of it. Kay obviously felt otherwise and his behaviour certainly did him no harm because he replaced Rob Lawton for the second Test in what was to be his one and only appearance for his country.

David Campese had been over to play for his Italian club between the two Tests and it seemed to have done him no harm whatsoever. Although Rory Underwood and Dean Richards scored tries for us, so did Campo . . . along with three of his team-mates. With Lynagh picking up 16 points, we suffered our third defeat by the Wallabies in less than 12 months – and our heaviest into the bargain.

Ironically, we had the best possible start by taking the lead with an Underwood try after only nine minutes. I had a hand in it too – arriving late from a lineout, missing the subsequent maul and then following the ball as Richard Harding spun it out wide. Will Carling slipped the ball back inside to me, and I linked with Jon Webb who sent Rory over. But then it all went wrong and on the evidence of Australia's 28–8 triumph, the gap between the home countries and the southern hemisphere seemed as wide as ever. In reality, however, with just a little luck and a shade more discipline we would have flown on to Fiji with a share of the series. Certainly there was no lack of team spirit and the general feeling was that the tide was beginning to turn England's way.

Fiji was tropical and sticky, with monsoon rains adding to the discomfort. The highlight of the match build-up – or lowlight, I should say – was the two-hour 'coach' trip from our training base in Nandi to our hotel in the capital Suva, where the Test was to be played at the National Stadium. Our transport was a real wreck . . . a charabanc with plastic seats and virtually no air-conditioning. But we just had to make the best of it.

It became clear as we travelled across the island – one of several hundred that make up the Fijian nation – just how passionate the people are about rugby. The kids in the parks were playing it instead of soccer and when we got to the hotel fans milled around begging for tickets. Although they are crazy about the game, many of them earn so little in a country of contrasting luxury and poverty that they simply cannot afford to buy tickets. Yet 25,000 still managed to find their way into the National Stadium for the Test showdown.

On the morning of the match England's police contingent of Dean Richards, John Bentley and myself were invited to local HQ to meet Suva's Chief of Police. We immediately found cava bowls thrust into our hands and were invited to join in the traditional welcoming ceremony. I'm convinced the intention was to nobble us for the big game . . . and it very nearly worked. Cava is basically a mild drug made from the roots of the pepper plant. The root is first crushed into a bowl with water or coconut milk and stirred thoroughly, after which the woody matter is removed. The ceremony involves a small wooden bowl of cava being drawn from a larger one, the host clapping and the guest responding before drinking the cava straight down. It tastes awful, like muddy water, but it numbs the lips, tongue and throat and after the first one you simply can't taste what you are drinking. After about three of these bowls, my head started to feel light, and when I left police HQ I swear I was floating above the pavement!

I'd still not come completely back down to earth when the England team arrived at the National Stadium, with its lone stand housing the changing-rooms and open grass banks all the way round. By the time we took the field and were introduced to the Fijian President, the stadium was packed with those 25,000 fanatical black faces. As I looked around I was still feeling the after-effects of my cava excesses and somewhat relieved I hadn't been drugs-tested.

We needed to finish the tour on a high note after our defeats in Australia but, knowing the Fijian reputation for brilliant handling throughout the team, were well aware of their unpredictability and the danger of giving them any chance to spin the ball. So, in conditions made treacherous by a monsoon downpour, we concentrated for the first 20 or 25 minutes on pounding away at their forwards. We rucked, mauled and drove them back, standing the man off and driving close again. It wasn't pretty to watch but the idea was to knock the stuffing out of them in their suspect departments – the physical confrontation up front and the set-piece play. The idea was not to give Severo Koroduadua, who was wearing the No. 10 shirt that day, any chance to get his back line moving.

The Fijians are always exceptionally fit and mobile and if they ever get their house in order and the right coach, they could well become as lethal at the 15-man game as they are at sevens. But while all their players are natural ball players they don't like the set-pieces or the physical stuff and that's where we had the beating of them. Just how much we had to be on our guard became evident on a couple of occasions when we drove them back towards their own line, only for the ball to spin loose because of the wet conditions. Suddenly the ball would be whipped like lightning through two or three pairs of Fijian hands and before we knew it we were back inside our own 25.

With the seconds ticking away, we were easing to a comfortable 25–12 victory when Gary Rees was pole-axed by Fijian prop Mosese Taga, who a year later was to get himself sent off at Twickenham for flattening Paul Ackford. The referee whistled for a penalty and as our team doctor came on to examine Rees's split lip, replacement Dave Egerton began to warm up on the touchline. 'Get on the pitch,' we urged him as the doctor led blood-spattered Rees off. The referee had already indicated there was barely enough time left to restart play, yet dithering Dave embarked on a meticulous stretching-off routine. Finally, he responded to our frantic calls and stepped on to the pitch . . . just as Stuart Barnes booted the penalty into touch and the whistle blew to end the game. The record books still show Egerton's third England cap as the shortest Test appearance of all time. He was on the field for precisely five seconds' play.

Prior to our arduous flight home via Sydney, a trip that was to take something like 35 hours, the tour ended with a poolside party at our hotel and the all-important players' court presided over by Paul Rendall. No tour was the same without the Judge's humorous summary convictions, incorporating punishments for the most innocuous offences from on-field playing indiscretions to players being offensive to the eye . . . or just plain boring. Even the management didn't escape the Judge's wrath and took what was coming to them in good part.

To assist in his running of the court, Paul would appoint counsel both for the defence and the prosecution. Brian Moore, as a solicitor in his own right, invariably filled the latter role which meant the defence counsel never quite got the same floor time as the prosecution! But the outcome would always be the same . . . guilty. Under Rendall, penalties and fines usually involved the consumption of a court cocktail or the dressing up of players in outrageous non-tour apparel. The players always had the final say, however, and it was the Judge and his court officials who found themselves in the dock on that last evening in Suva.

The Players' Revolutionary Court duly decided on a suitable punishment to fit his 'crime'. The Judge, unanimously convicted of over-exuberance in his sentencing throughout the tour, was ordered to spend the evening dressed as a dusky Fijian maiden – complete with boot-polish face, pink permed wig, straw bra and grass skirt.

CHAPTER EIGHT

Poms Away

AFTER three defeats by Australia in 12 months, I finally sampled the taste of beating the Wallabies later in 1988. In fact the delight was actually doubled, because it happened twice in 18 days! A couple of months after we returned from Down Under, Nick Farr-Jones and his men came to Britain for a tour that included Tests against ourselves and Scotland. However, unlike Andy Slack's 1984 Grand Slammers, they were brought back to earth – in a rugby sense at least – almost as soon as their flight touched down at Heathrow.

Their opening game, a Twickenham date with Dick Best's London Division, saw them suffer a humiliating 21–10 defeat. It also brought a hitherto unsung lock by the name of Paul Ackford to the forefront. He had been on the club and divisional scenes for some years and had actually played for England B back in 1979 when I was still dreaming of a Lancashire cap. But he was a new name to me in 1988 although that was to change dramatically over the next few weeks as, on the strength of his London performance, he leapfrogged into the England team as my new second-row partner.

In the meantime Australia's problems went from bad to worse as they were humbled by both the North and South West divisional sides. I was in the line-up when the North triumphed 15–9 at Otley and so was another player who was about to complete a meteoric rise to international level. Just three months earlier, Dewi Morris had been playing for Cheshire junior club, Winnington Park. Then the Welsh-born scrum-half joined Liverpool St Helens, made a try-scoring debut in that North victory, and did so well for England B against the Aussies four days later that, like Ackford, he was drafted in for his first senior cap.

By the time we got round to the Test match a couple of weeks later, the tourists had also been thumped 26–10 by the South West, so most of the England boys now had personal experience of winning against Australia. The Aussies would, of course, have claimed the divisional sides had only beaten their Wednesday team, but nevertheless the victories gave us extra confidence under our newly-appointed skipper Will Carling and helped to lift us above the mediocrity and inconsistency that had held England rugby back for years.

Geoff Cooke's decision to hand the captaincy to Carling five weeks before his 23rd birthday came as quite a surprise to some of the more senior players. It was certainly a bold move to appoint such an inexperienced player to the job at a time when most of us felt an older head like Rob Andrew or Brian Moore would have been a more suitable choice. Those two were certainly not averse to speaking their minds at team meetings, whilst Will appeared extremely young to be thrust into such a responsible position.

As events turned out, the choice of Carling proved a master stroke and he quickly went up in my estimation by showing his preparedness to turn to senior players for advice. The fact that he is so willing to listen is, in my opinion, one of the reasons why he has been such a successful captain. Although he was still comparatively raw in England terms when he took over the reins, he demonstrated from the start that he was prepared to take advantage of the knowledge and experience he had around him.

As the pressure mounted, he also came through impressively in other aspects of the job. He managed to cope effectively with his own high-profile image, the attentions of the media and, at one point, personal loss of form and speculation that he was not worth his place as a player. It was not really until the following season that we realised what a good choice of captain the management had made. As everyone now knows Will developed into a genuine world-class player, providing testimony to the inspired thinking that prompted Geoff to appoint him in the first place.

We began the Test against Australia with three new caps – Ackford, Morris and Harlequins wing Andy Harriman – and finished with a fourth when Carling went off concussed and John Buckton took over. By then the Wallabies were a beaten side and Ackers and I had struck up an understanding that was to go from strength to strength over the next three seasons. At 30, Paul was a late starter at this level, but he was a natural. An out-and-out No. 4 jumper like myself, he was forced because of my presence in the team to start again at the front of the lineout; and he adapted exceptionally well. So well in fact that he developed very quickly into one of the best front jumpers in the world.

He also took a great deal of pressure off me, because up to that point I had been England's main ball winner. Now I had someone to share the role, and we soon discovered that we were complementing each other with devastating effect. As fellow policemen we also found we had a great deal in common off the pitch, and although Paul was an inspector and I a constable, we quickly became good friends. After all, I was senior-ranking *on* the field!

Although that was his first game for England, Ackers was a vastly experienced player and it really showed through on the day. Mind you, he did finish up completely knackered by the final whistle! Buoyed by the knowledge that the Aussies were beatable, we took them on up front . . . and took them apart. Yet for most of the game we simply could not get away from them in terms of points. Every time we scored they would claw their way back, just as they had done in the ill-fated Brisbane Test earlier in the year. However, when Carling finally sent Simon Halliday in for our fourth try we stretched away, still full of running, to win 28–19.

The aura of southern hemisphere invincibility had been wiped out. We had finally put one over them and, equally important, our fitness methods were working. It was November 5, 1988 . . . and the spark that was to set England rugby alight had been ignited.

Our victory was put into better perspective when the Aussies ran up 211 points in winning the last six games of the tour, including a 32–13 victory against Scotland and 40–22 romp against a Barbarians side in which I was on a loser from the start. It was another defeat in my chronicle of disastrous results in Cardiff, only this time I did have an excuse. Because of work commitments I went into the game with just a couple of hours' preparation after driving down from Blackpool on the morning of the match. Arriving so late I was scarcely in a position to dictate where I played and I found myself jumping at the front of the line with Bob Norster in the middle. Before the game the forwards ran through a few lineouts on the big indoor practice area at the Arms Park, and that was just about all the preparation I had.

Against an improving team with the unity of a full tour behind them we faced an uphill climb from the start and they finished their visit on a high note. When it was all over I did not even have the pleasure of staying for the after-match reception. Since I was working the following day, I had to head home straight after the game.

By now England were almost into the 1989 Five Nations season, and after our victory over the Aussies we were confident of a good Championship. However, the champagne immediately went flat when we blew our Triple Crown chances with a 12–12 draw against the Scots at Twickenham. It was a bad start, particularly as we had the majority of the game, but to our credit we immediately bounced back to beat Ireland 16–3 in Dublin before seeing off the French at home, 11–0.

That game was my first insight into the cunning tactical substitutions France have introduced into their strategy in recent years. Although it's illegal, it happens far too often for the 'injuries' to be genuine and they seem to get away with it every time. On this occasion their prop Portolan was having a particularly hard time and midway through the first half they were on the rack near their own line. When we pushed them back they collapsed so we promptly picked them up again and Paul Rendall popped Portolan out of the scrum. The next minute, for no reason at all, he developed a limp . . . and off he went to be replaced by the more experienced Jean-Pierre Garuet. There was absolutely nothing wrong with Portolan; somewhere along the line someone had given him the wink. Things weren't going well for the tight five so they simply substituted him.

My understanding with Ackers was developing all the time, and the critics attributed both those victories to our ball-winning success. One report said after the Ireland game: 'Ackford and Dooley completely dominated the lineout and the flood of ball from this source completely dictated the game.' And the way we disposed of the French merited the following comment: 'England, through the superb jumping of Ackford and Dooley, achieved a lineout superiority that would have turned the All Blacks green with envy.'

Whatever the influence of Paul and myself, the indisputable fact was the team were starting to string wins together and to gel as a unit. Suddenly we were within one game of our first Championship for nine years . . . still unbeaten and strongly fancied to achieve it by beating the rapidly deteriorating Welsh at Cardiff.

Instead, we managed to blow it although I will always be convinced Mike Teague's early injury was a crucial factor, since it deprived me of a key lineout support man. Much of my success over the years has been down to my support players – from Teague and Rendall to Micky Skinner and Jason Leonard – and to lose a player of Mike's pedigree in the first minute cut my options right down. The man who replaced him, Gary Rees, just isn't a lineout support player. He's an out-and-out openside flanker whose natural position is at the back of the line. The end product was that I could not get any sort of grip on the lineouts; and to make matters worse Norster played out of his skin. If anybody won the game for the Welsh that day it was the combination of Norster's lineout work and Robert Jones with his superb tactical kicking in the rain. Yet it could well have been a totally different story but for that injury to Teague.

That game had an added significance: it was my final chance to prove my credentials for the British Lions tour of Australia that summer. Although I had been confident all along of being chosen as one of the four locks in the squad, I was hoping to oust Norster as number one for the middle-of-the-line job in the Test matches. The Wales game had provided the ideal platform to prove my point but with half my support missing and Norster jumping like a dream, I blew my big chance.

I couldn't even blame the conditions because Bob was taking the ball two-handed at times! Ackford found it just as tough at the front, where Phil Davies spent all afternoon taking him out of the line. It was very effective, too, and nullified the controlled lineout ball which had enabled England to do so well throughout the championship. It was also one of the few occasions when Paul and I were cleaned out as a pair by the opposition.

Another Five Nations season had begun with much promise and finished with no reward, and there was still another hurdle to surmount before the Lions set off for Australia. The RFU, in all its wisdom, had fixed up a first-ever trip to Bucharest to play Romania in May. Nicolae Ceausescu was still at the height of his powers and, before we set out, London-based Romanian journalist Chris Thau was invited to the Petersham Hotel to tell us what to expect. The prospect was not exactly mouth-watering . . . and I don't mean just the food. We were advised to be careful where we went, where we talked and what we discussed because Securitate ears were everywhere and there was every chance our hotel rooms would be bugged. It was also suggested we take our own food, along with commodities like tea and coffee, because the Romanian equivalents left a lot to be desired.

We flew out to Bucharest accompanied by two large chests full of food – one for ourselves and one for the Under-21 squad which was accompanying us. The chef at our hotel must have thought it was his birthday! Flying with the Romanian national airline, Tarom, was scarcely a five-star experience. In fact it was more like travelling on an old bus than a plane and on the flight back I noticed that some of the seats had actually been hand-painted!

It was sweltering in Bucharest and on the first night we were treated to an example of local cuisine. The meal the hotel served up was dreadful and we quickly realised why the RFU had decided to supplement our diet with food brought from England. The coffee was black and horrible, the meat minimal and like leather, and the salad comprised limp lettuce and little else. In that heat we needed extra nourishment to get us through training, yet the portions were totally inadequate and we had to ask for them to be increased.

On our first evening, some of us naively decided to take a stroll down the street and try to find a bar. We turned right outside the hotel and wandered down towards the government buildings. There was virtually no one around, apart from the suspicious grey-suited characters who stood in pairs on almost every street corner. We walked for around quarter-of-a-mile and were followed every step of the way by shadowy figures. Then, accepting that there were no bars and absolutely nothing worth seeing, we turned round . . . and were followed all the way back to the hotel. It was only around 9 p.m., yet there were so few people around that you could have been excused for thinking the government had imposed a curfew on people leaving their homes.

Even down at the British Embassy the diplomats didn't feel safe. The staff put on a garden party for us and although the ambassador himself was away, his wife explained that they never discussed anything private within the walls of the embassy for fear of the place being bugged. They just did not know which of the local staff they could trust.

The beauty of some of the old villas and public buildings made it easy to appreciate why Bucharest was once known as the Paris of the East. In contrast, Ceausescu's regime had imposed its grey, miserable legacy across the city in the shape of characterless tower blocks and drab, half-empty shops full of outdated merchandise. There also seemed to be precious little for the people to do . . . apart from queueing for food.

Aware of the awful conditions the locals had to endure, Dean Richards, myself and one or two of the other lads strolled down to the local market on the morning of the game, where we saw the queues at first hand. There was very little food to queue for, either. It was all so sad, particularly as the people themselves were so friendly.

The temperature must have been 90 degrees inside the August 23 Stadium, an open-air concrete bowl named after the day the Soviet communists 'freed' the country in 1944. The Under-21s had to play in the full heat of the early afternoon and how they came through those 80 sweltering minutes I don't know. Even more staggering was the perform-ance of young Neil Back. The Leicester flanker was a revelation; he just didn't stop running all afternoon. While he was flying about everywhere, we sat around in the shade taking in as much liquid as possible, and trying to conserve our energy for the big game, which followed at 5 p.m.

It was still very hot when we kicked off and, bearing in mind that the Romanians had beaten Wales, Scotland and France in the same stadium in recent years, we expected a tough time. Instead, it was a rout; we just took them apart and I was amazed how easy it was. It wasn't so much that they played badly, more that we turned on some superb stuff and never allowed them to get into the game. They lost the forward battle comprehensively, so they tried to open it up with any scraps of possession they poached. But although they had some handy backs, they just got nowhere and we finished up winning by the record margin of 58–3.

I exchanged shirts at the end with my opposite number but I didn't have his jersey for long. As I headed for the changing-room a young boy eyed it up longingly through the railings from outside the ground – one of many fans who appeared to have been locked out because they could not afford the entrance fee. Just to see the look of utter joy on the boy's face when I gave him Sandu Ciorascu's shirt made it all worthwhile. There could not have been more than 10,000 people inside the ground for the game . . . yet there seemed to be almost as many milling around outside behind the railings.

Back at the hotel, prior to leaving for the airport to fly home, we all collected together our remaining tea, coffee, sugar and other commodities and presented the sizeable package to the chambermaids who had looked after us so well during our stay. They thought it was absolutely wonderful; far more acceptable than any amount of money.

Our own particular maid, who was in her forties, had spent the week eyeing Paul Rendall's old pair of Nike training shoes. Although they had seen better days, that particular item of well-worn footwear had seen the Judge through numerous bleep tests and not surprisingly he thought the world of them. He had also had them adapted because of an achilles problem, but the maid's pleading eyes proved more compelling than Paul's sentimental attachment. Her need, I decided, was greater than his – or at least the need of her husband or son. The Judge was left totally mystified when his frantic search failed to reveal the missing shoes. Finally accepting that he would never see them again, he admitted defeat and it was not until we were well on our way home that I came clean and told him the truth. I had given his beloved trainers to the maid. Paul was livid and I couldn't really blame him. But eventually he managed to raise a smile at the thought of a middle-aged Romanian chambermaid racing along the dimly-lit hotel corridor with his tatty pair of trainers on her feet . . . and her arms full of tea and coffee.

CHAPTER NINE

Pride and Prejudice: the 1989 Lions

THE 1989 British Lions were on a winner from the moment we met for our pre-tour get-together at the Oaklands Hotel in Surrey. The weekend message of goodwill from tour manager Clive Rowlands was simple: 'Go out, get drunk and enjoy yourselves!'

Clive had managed the Lions team for the International Board centenary games back in 1986, and I knew from then that he was a guy who had the welfare of his players very much at heart. The first task at the Oaklands was to blend together a squad of players from four rival countries who were more used to being in opposition – antagonists rather than team-mates. The cancellation for political reasons of the 1986 trip to South Africa meant there had been no official Lions tour for six years; so apart from the odd Barbarians game, most of us had had little experience of playing together.

However, we had in Rowlands, coaches Ian McGeechan and Roger Uttley, and skipper Finlay Calder as good a quartet of leaders as we could possibly have asked for. Anyone who has met Geech and Roger knows what genuine, likeable guys they are, while every one of the players had the utmost respect for the Fin as a worthy captain. The back-room team was completed by Ben Gilfeather, the Scot who as England's team doctor had a foot in two camps, and physio Kevin Murphy, who has always been a star man in his own right.

If any of us were strangers to each other when we arrived for that break-the-ice weekend, it certainly wasn't for long. Any barriers that might have existed between English, Irish, Scottish and Welsh factions were quickly broken down and a squad policy introduced that, wherever possible, players from the same country would never room together, and forwards would be paired up with backs. By the time we went our separate ways at the end of the weekend, kitted out for the challenge ahead, the 1989 Lions were roaring a single tune.

Shortly before flying out to Australia, we had a second pre-tour get-together at the Oaklands to undergo fitness tests – including the dreaded bleep test. Unfortunately, my grandfather Bill had died a few days before, and was cremated on the day the Lions were due to meet. He and I had been very close, and although he was never well enough to travel to Twickenham for internationals, he had followed my rugby career closely and watched all the big games avidly on TV. I spent the early part of that day in the village of Walton attending the funeral, proudly wearing my new Lions blazer. The last thing I did before leaving for London was to take my grandfather's old griffin dog, Vic, for a last walk around the village, where I had spent some happy times as a youngster. Finally I said my goodbyes to the rest of the family and set off to team up with the squad.

When I arrived at the Oaklands around tea-time, hardly in the best frame of mind, Finlay Calder was waiting at the front door in the sunshine. Presumably his intention was to take my mind off events earlier in the day, but I was certainly not prepared for what followed. While I had been at the funeral, the other boys had all done their bleep tests and Fin's instruction was: 'Be ready at 5.30. We'll do your test outside the hotel.'

This is a wind-up, I thought, smiling to myself as I went up to my room to unpack before stretching out on the bed for a rest. A little later the phone rang with the message I wasn't really expecting. 'The course is set up outside the hotel. Your presence is required.'

I went downstairs in running shorts and tee-shirt to find the other boys milling around on the grass verge outside the hotel having a drink. It *was* a joke, I decided, ordering myself a pint of lager and polishing it off swiftly. Halfway through my second pint, the truth dawned on me. The test was for real . . . and the boys had launched a £5-a-go sweepstake on what level I would reach!

Roger Uttley had measured out a course on the grass and a car had been parked alongside to play the tape. It was a beautiful day and a beautiful setting – and the other players weren't expecting too much from me. It's a major challenge doing the bleep test at any time, but with a pint and a half of lager on board, most of the lads reckoned I'd get through the first couple of levels and then collapse. That's where the big money went, with the odd exception like Irish hooker Steve Smith, who went for something totally outrageous and backed me to reach level 14.

I set off on the test, cheered on – or rather jeered on – by the other players, with Gareth Chilcott and Roger strategically placed to see I touched the line at each end of the course. Over the next ten minutes or so I staggered everyone, not least myself, because I recorded my best performance ever. I was officially clocked at level 14 plus three 20-yard lengths and it earned Smithy a handsome £65 pay-off. I never did get my £32.50.

Whether the course was short, the tape slow or my performance was enhanced by the lager, I don't know. But I promised myself that the next time I took a bleep test I'd do my utmost to pay a visit to a local hostelry beforehand! I'm not sure if putting me through the test that evening was a bit of psychology on Fin's part or just entertainment for the troops. But it certainly worked, taking my mind off family matters and focusing it back on the job in hand.

It also showed that I had never been fitter, which was a legacy of the great amount of work I had put in once the squad was named. Although it was fairly obvious I was going to Australia as No. 2 to Bob Norster, I had set my mind from the start on winning a Test place and my dedication to that cause was clearly paying off. In fact the overall efforts of the England players in the tour build-up had also paid off well because in that bleep test the two players who came out on top were myself and Brian Moore.

Just about the only friction on the entire tour came during our first couple of training sessions. As skipper, Finlay naturally had a major say in forward training and he and the other Scots wanted to play the out-and-out rucking game in which they specialised. But while Fin, John Jeffrey, David Sole and Co. were happy to race around launching themselves head first into tackle bags, the rest of the forwards wanted to incorporate the mauling approach as well. The way they trained left everybody susceptible to neck injuries, but it was really the only way they knew. The emphasis of their game was on speed and mobility, but they weren't particularly strong in the upper body and relied basically on firing around everywhere at 100 miles-an-hour, driving head-first into the opposition. A compromise was needed, and we quickly found the right formula. The tackle-bag drills were moderated, and we settled for an approach allowing us to incorporate both types of game. From then on, we were all pulling in the same direction . . . and it developed into one of the happiest tours of my career.

We arrived in Australia, the first British Lions team to tour the country for 23 years, conscious of the adverse treatment and results some of the home union sides had experienced Down Under – and determined to prove that, contrary to popular belief among the Aussies, there *was* rugby played outside the southern hemisphere. We were complete underdogs, written off by the media, but I was convinced we had a squad capable of doing well. As it turned out, the Australian Press was the best thing that could have happened to us. They turned against us virtually from day one, and if anything had an influence in pulling the side together it was them.

The vitriol began even before our first game against Western Australia in Perth. A local cameraman wanted a photograph of our three policemen forwards, Paul Ackford, Dean Richards and myself, for a national newspaper, and while we were happy to oblige it was suggested to him that he might like to make a small donation to the tour fund. There was nothing underhand about it, no demand for money and no question of us refusing to co-operate if he didn't pay. It is accepted practice for players to organise a small fund, incorporating things like tour court fines and sale of souvenir tee-shirts, to provide a kitty for the odd round of drinks and other incidentals.

The Aussie pressman was taken aback by the suggestion. 'Oh, I don't know about that,' he said. 'I'll have to ask my editor.' He duly took his photos, went off happily with them and we thought no more of it. The following day, however, the headline in that particular paper read something like: LIONS PLAYERS DEMAND MONEY FOR INTER-VIEWS. The story went off into the realms of fantasy, claiming we had refused to be photographed unless money was handed over. The war of words had started and as a result all future Press interviews with the players were directed through and cleared by the management.

Despite media excesses, the Australian public in general were very hospitable and appreciative of the ambassadorial work we did in visiting rugby clubs and schools, attending charity dinners and other PR exercises. The warm way we were welcomed was highlighted before our first game when the players took part in a race around the bay as guests of the local yacht club in Perth. It's just as well that didn't cost anything because some of the boys had already blown their tour allowance in the Burswood casino resort where we were staying.

We had a week to prepare for the first match, and training started in earnest. The great thing about Ian McGeechan's sessions was that while they were hard and physical they were always varied and extremely enjoyable. With the canny Scotsman no two sessions were alike.   He had this great knack of keeping the players interested *and* in prime condition – and you could see why the Scots boys held him in such high esteem.

By the time the opening game against Western Australia came around, we were raring to go. We were unsure of what to expect because their team reportedly included a good number of ex-pat New Zealanders. It was a sweltering day and as things turned out a bit of a mismatch because they were a poor side and we scored nine tries in swamping them 44–0. Mismatch or not, it was an exceptionally good start . . . even if my own contribution was somewhat meagre. I spent the afternoon sitting in the stand eating ice cream!

There was, however, a worrying development in that we lost our No. 1 fly-half, Irishman Paul Dean, with an ankle injury which was to end his international career. Despite desperate efforts to restore him to fitness, Dean was eventually flown home for an operation . . . to be replaced by Rob Andrew. It had surprised me that Rob had not been included in the squad in the first place, and he emphasised the point by becoming one of the biggest successes of the series.

In the early stages of the tour, it was policy to give everybody a game and look at different combinations with a view to the forthcoming Tests. Bob Norster and Donal Lenihan were teamed up in the second row for the Perth game, but four days later it was Paul Ackford and myself who turned out against a very strong Australia B side in Melbourne. Weary from the long flight from one side of the country to the other, playing conditions could not have been more different after the blazing sunshine of Perth. At times we were ankle deep in mud . . . and my tour almost came to a sticky end right there. Towards the end of the game Tim Horan hit me in the tackle low, hard and from the side – and the conditions, combined with the contact, twisted my left knee. Although I didn't know it until later I had torn the cruciate ligament. In a dour forward battle the packs swopped pushover tries and we ran out eventual winners, 23–18.

I knew my injury wasn't as bad as the one that had crippled me back in 1986, but both physio Kevin Murphy and I feared the damage was reasonably serious. However, I knew I had to get back playing as soon as possible. There was no way the tour management would wait indefinitely for me to recover and the big worry was that if I was laid up for more than a few days they would send for a replacement and put me on a flight back to England.

Thankfully a combination of intensive treatment by Kevin and strapping up the knee for training led to the mobility gradually returning. As things turned out, I carried that injury right through the tour, although it proved to be nowhere near as troublesome as I had first feared.

On our R and R stop in Cairns, Gareth Chilcott and I, as members of the entertainment committee, organised a day out for the boys white-water rafting on the Barren River. It was a pretty hairy experience, both exhilarating and frightening at the same time . . . and it almost cost David Young his life. There were five of us in each boat, plus a guide, and we were tossed all over the place as we shot through the rapids. About half-way down was an outcrop of rock on the right, at which point we were meant to keep to the left. To emphasise the danger the guides had strung a safety rope across the river just before the rocks in case anyone got into difficulties. Our crew managed to manoeuvre clear of trouble, but one of the later boats containing Roger Uttley, Mike Teague, Derek White, Rory Underwood and Young went to the right and capsized. They immediately found themselves in major difficulties, particularly Dai . . . because he couldn't swim! The poor guy thought his number was up at one point but he was eventually dragged to safety by the guide. Typical prop, white-water rafting without his water wings. He might as well have gone skydiving without a parachute or bungi jumping without a rope! Cooch and I came in for a fair bit of stick afterwards, I can tell you.

I knew that if I was to have any chance of making the Test team I had to play in the next midweek game against Queensland B. So, knee heavily strapped, I struggled out with Lenihan's Wednesday side on a wet evening in Cairns . . . and scored a try in a 30–6 triumph. Having started the move from a lineout on the far right I was grateful to accept the final pass to dive in under the posts. That game was sandwiched between the two 'mini Tests' against Queensland and New South Wales. Whilst I was not fit enough to be considered for the Queensland game, which we won 19–15, this proved to be an ill-tempered affair with both sides guilty at times of over-robust play. Yet it was some of the Queensland players and officials who took it upon themselves to cry foul play. The writing was beginning to appear on the wall.

With the Aussie media taking up the cudgel, the attacks became more and more frenzied as the tour progressed. Why did they do it? I honestly believe they were very nervous about the outcome of the series. They could see we were a happy, close-knit unit with capable players and no in-fighting, yet they desperately wanted to help their own side.

The only way they could do that was by laying into us and trying to discredit us in any way they could, be it for negative or violent play, or whatever. Yet all it did was pull us even closer together!

The continuing selection of Norster and Ackford for the big games was an ominous sign for my Test chances. I watched from the stand as the boys pipped New South Wales 23–21 in a real nailbiter at North Sydney Oval. Donal's Doughnuts were conceived prior to the next midweek match – a date with NSW B before the big one on the Saturday. But motivation was no problem. The Wednesday team is as much part of a tour as the Test side itself . . . and of course we were keen to maintain the Lions' 100 per cent tour record. Although I was disappointed not to have made the senior line-up, I was enjoying my part as a member of the Doughnuts. Apart from anything else, it meant we were able to relax in the build-up to the big Saturday matches. We would all go out after the midweek game and concentrate on our other great challenge . . . to seek out every Guinness pub in Australia. The social side was excellent, and skipper Lenihan had a dual role in that he was tour Judge – the man who presided over our improvised team courts. The Cork bank official's dry Irish humour made him an apt choice for the job.

Paul Ackford partnered me against New South Wales B in a side which included seven men who were to play in the Test three days later – and we made it six tour wins out of six with a comfortable 39–19 victory. While Norster and Ackford were predictably chosen as the lock pairing for the first Test, the rest of the line-up was not altogether what we expected. With Mike Teague still recovering from a shoulder injury received against New South Wales, the biggest surprise was the selection of Derek White as a flanker – particularly as he had played all his previous tour games at No. 8.

As I took my seat in the capacity crowd at the impressive Sydney Football Stadium, my frustration at missing out was tempered by the fact that there was a good reason for it. The boys had been playing exceptionally well up front, with a brand of imposing, driving forward play led in the main by Teague and David Sole.

The game was preceded by a rendition of *Advance Australia Fair* which sounded very patriotic and meaningful. But since most of the Aussie crowd didn't know the words of the anthem, they were screened on the electronic scoreboard and printed in the programme.

Despite the absence of Teague and injured centres Scott Hastings and John Devereux, I felt we had every chance of winning. Instead, the wheels came off the victory band-wagon in disastrous fashion. The Wallabies, playing in front of one of the biggest crowds to watch a Rugby Union game in Australia for many a year, played out of their skins and took us apart. We were walloped 30–12, and a try count of 4–0 emphasised their superiority. The Lions never seemed able to grasp hold of the game in what was the first lacklustre performance up front of the tour. We were made to look very ordinary in all departments and the Aussie lineout presence of Steve Cutler, Bill Campbell, Steve Tuynman and Scott Gourley reigned supreme. We had a week to sort this big problem area out and from my personal point of view, the significant factor was that Norster had a very average game and was wiped out in the lineout by Cutler. Bob's demise was not something I would wish on anyone, but suddenly I felt I was in with a shout for the second Test.

The Lions' changing-room after the game was a picture of desolation. The boys were absolutely distraught, and there was little we non-combatants could do to relieve the misery. Yet in a strange way that defeat – and the flak it sparked from the Press both at home and in Australia – was probably good for the tour, uniting us more than ever and stiffening our resolve to win the series. At the same time, a golden opportunity was knocking for me personally and I had no intention of wasting it.

The midweek game at Canberra against Australian Capital Territories was fraught with danger. They had a reputation similar to the North Division in England for toppling touring sides and by half-time we knew exactly why. Serenaded every time they scored by a scratchy rendering of a kookaburra song over the public address system, by the end of the first half they had stormed into a 21–11 lead. So we had already heard that record once too often. The tour was at the crossroads; a second successive defeat would have been devastating, particularly with the second Test just days away. We *had* to turn it round and ram that kookaburra back down their throats – and we did it so effectively that we won the game 41–25. We took control up front with a combination of tight forward play and pressure on the ACT defensive scrummage; and Peter Dods's boot completed the job as he finished up with 21 points. It was a second-half performance of real guts and character, led manfully by skipper Lenihan. The Doughnuts had got the show back on the road.

I knew my first-half try and overall performance had done my Test chances no harm, but when I took another knock on my suspect knee I feared the worst. I needn't have worried. Smurf got down to more heroics with the physiotherapy over the next couple of days and when the team sheet went up for the Brisbane Test, there alongside Ackford in the second row was the name DOOLEY.

Although he didn't show it, the news must have been as shattering for Bob as it was exhilarating for me. It was a major coup to have ousted the man who had for so long been a thorn in my side at international level, and if I had my way he wasn't going to get his place back. This was my big chance to prove I could perform on a world stage, and I had every reason to feel confident since I had a reasonably good record against Cutler. With five Englishmen in the pack, including fit again Mike Teague, I also had the benefit of a familiar support team around me.

At our final team meeting just before the game, Roger went through his routine of picking out forwards individually for a few pre-match words. When he got to me, he did wonders for my confidence by announcing: 'Wade, you are replacing one of the best lineout jumpers in Europe. He's athletic, mobile, aggressive, his timing is perfection itself . . . and you're in because you're big.' How that was meant to motivate me I don't know, but the ridiculousness of the comment didn't register at the time as my mind was focused on the game ahead. The other players struggled to keep straight faces, especially Teague, who had shared another amusing moment involving Roger and me before the French game at Twickenham a few months earlier. On that occasion Uttley had told me: 'Wade, you're a bit of an enigma.' He was actually referring to playing my club rugby in the Fourth Division but after the meeting I asked Mike: 'What the hell's an enigma?' I was delighted when he confirmed Roger meant it as a tribute. 'I think it's a high-performance Japanese motor-bike.' he announced. We both cracked up . . . and to this day I still get ribbed about those weird Uttley assessments of my playing qualities.

Basically, my brief was to get into Cutler's ribs and give him a hard time. The idea was to put the gangling New South Welshman off his game – and that is precisely what I did. We had decided before the match that our best chance of victory was to keep it tight and concentrate on establishing forward dominance.

We were one Test down, and we had to play some hard, physical rugby; we had to take them on up front and slow down their pack. As it turned out the tactics worked a treat. After some early lively rucking by both sides, the Lions gained the upper hand with devastating rolling mauls in which Teague was outstanding. The frustrated Aussies reacted by trying to confront us head-on, and still they came off worse. Nevertheless, a Greg Martin try and some deadly kicking by Michael Lynagh ensured we were never in front at any stage until late in the second half when Gavin Hastings stormed in to put us 13–12 ahead. Then, to rub in our superiority, Jerry Guscott stretched the final score to 19–12 with a moment of sheer brilliance, chipping through before touching down with that air of arrogance all class players have.

One regrettable moment was the stamping of Cutler by Young. Admittedly, Dai might have been sent off for it and indeed he was reprimanded by our own management afterwards. But the Press, not prepared to leave it there, went absolutely hysterical – not only about the Young incident but also in their condemnation of our so-called softening-up tactics. There were whingeing Wallabies, too, notably Farr-Jones, Campbell and hooker Tom Lawton . . . and when they joined the attack, we knew the series was there for the taking.

That second Test also contained a couple of bouts of fisticuffs among the forwards, sparked when scrum-halves Robert Jones and Nick Farr-Jones squared up like two schoolgirls slapping each other. Robert was accused not only of stamping on Farr-Jones's boot, but also grinding his studs into his foot. Yet it was certainly not an overtly dirty game, even if the Aussie Press were so incensed by their team's defeat that they laid into us from every angle. They even resorted to a disgraceful libellous attack on the three policemen in the Lions pack – myself, Richards and Ackford.

One reporter referred to 'licensed thuggery' by English police officers, while another wrote: 'In the convict days, the British bullies applied the lash to the wild colonial boys. Two hundred years later, the British bulldog is still whipping us and kicking us around. Perhaps significantly, three members of the aggressive and dominant British pack are members of the constabulary. They did to the Wallabies what they do to Pakistanis and punks back home.'

That type of comment left such a nasty taste that the three of us sought advice whether to pursue a legal action. These people were not merely having a go at our rugby; the slurs were aimed at our jobs, our families and everything we stood for back home. However, the final Test was just a few days away and the last thing we wanted was a distraction. That was exactly what these people wanted . . . to put us off our game. Let's get the facts straight about that second Test. Nothing was pre-planned apart from the fact we were going to take the Wallabies on up front and play more of a driving, forward-orientated game. The idea was purely to suck in their forwards and starve them of as much possession as we could. As for Aussie suggestions that a '99' call went up the moment the scrum-half scrap started, that is absolute rubbish. We simply stood up from the scrummage, saw two guys fighting and with Robert surrounded by the opposition naturally reacted to defend our team-mate.

In his autobiography, David Campese suggests we went out with the express intention of trying to intimidate the opposition and knock the hell out of them. That comment is typical of the hysteria we had to put up with at the time; but the fact is that if we did knock the hell out of them it was done strictly within the laws of the game – barring that one unfortunate incident with Young.

The plan for the third Test at Sydney Football Stadium was the same. In front of yet another capacity crowd who were there to witness the final showdown, Teague was again in superb form and we got some tremendous drives on in the first quarter which rocked the Aussies back on their heels. We never really allowed them to get into the game, only for Ian Williams to snap up a try on just about the first occasion they looked like scoring. The move was inspired by Lynagh, who opened up our defence brilliantly in the centre to put Williams away on the outside. The books were to be balanced, however, by a bizarre mistake from Campese that ultimately cost Australia the series. For some reason known only to himself, he tried to run the ball out from behind his own line, and when his pass outside to Greg Martin went astray, Ieuan Evans dived on the ball for what proved to be the decisive score. The crowd couldn't believe it, we couldn't believe it, Ieuan couldn't believe it . . . and certainly Martin couldn't believe it.

It was typical outrageous Campese; one minute the genius the next the clown. If he had done it again, the pass would probably have gone to hand and he'd have ended up scoring at the other end. Having said that, if he had concentrated more on what he was doing *on* the park instead of what he was saying off it, perhaps he might have won the game for them instead of losing it! He certainly was not in the best of moods for the rest of the game. At one point I caught him marginally late with my shoulder as he cleared the ball. We exchanged a few pleasantries – and his embarrassment and frustration were pretty evident.

Even at 19–12 in the lead, we managed to give them a lifeline by conceding a couple of silly penalties to Lynagh. Finlay Calder was pulled up for handling on the floor, then Teague went over the top in front of our own posts and suddenly we were hanging on by a single point at 19–18. It was desperate stuff now but, significantly, when the final whistle came we had them penned in their own half, pressuring the home try-line.

It was one of the greatest moments of my career. Just to be part of a British Lions side is something special but to be a member of a series-winning team when the odds are stacked against you, well, that is something else. Although we had won all our other matches, let's face it, when the record books are written nobody remembers the provincial games. It's the Tests that are all-important. In a hostile atmosphere, we had our backs to the wall after losing the first Test, yet we survived hostility all around us to win the next two with a combination of courage, conviction and commitment.

The celebrations started at the final whistle and went on long into the night. Clive Rowlands personally saw every player off the park, and when we met up with the boys who had been sitting in the stands it was sheer euphoria all round as the champagne overflowed.

The support for the Lions throughout the tour had been absolutely fantastic, culminating in what appeared to be a 50 per cent British contingent at the Test matches. As our way of saying thank-you we went back out for a lap of honour – to an incredible reception. It was such an emotional experience that I got carried away blowing a kiss to the crowd. Needless to say the boys spotted it on the video afterwards and I was hauled before Judge Lenihan . . . and fined heavily for being an English poofter!

When we arrived at the official dinner that night, the stairs and the landing of the hotel were awash with celebrating Brits. We trooped in off the coach to an incredible reception and from then on my recollections of the evening are distinctly dim. I suspect a surfeit of alcohol may have had something to do with it . . .

Although I had managed to carry my knee through the Test, I wasn't fit enough to play in the two games that rounded off the tour, against an NSW Country XV and the Anzacs. Paul Ackford also thought his tour was over since he had played more games than anyone else, so – expecting Lenihan and Norster to do the business against the Anzacs – the two of us spent a highly enjoyable few days on the beer. It was the worst thing Paul could have done because it was *he*, not Lenihan, who was picked to partner Norster in that farewell game in Brisbane. Perhaps it would have been better had his wife Susie not gone home after we clinched the series.

Susie had arrived just before the Brisbane Test and, showing remarkable bravery, actually dared to return to the hotel from Ballymore on the team bus, accompanying the euphoric, somewhat raucous squad members. She paid for it though, because the boys decided that, like the rest of us, she had to have her own official tour number. While we were numbered from one to 31, poor Susie had to put up with the embarrassment of being appointed the British Lions' No. 69!

The real class act of the tour was Mike Teague. The big West Country builder was officially named Man of the Series for his phenomenal performances and no one could dispute his right to the award. Not bad for a daft Gloucester brickie!

Despite having represented the Lions in the 1986 IRFB Centenary celebrations, I discovered in Australia that there is nothing quite like a British Lions tour. Competing and striving for a Test place alongside the best players the UK has to offer, within an alien squad environment, is a totally different entity to travelling abroad with your home union.

The challenge of moulding the diverse characters and playing styles of the other nations into a cohesive unit both on and off the pitch was a highly rewarding experience that will stay with me for a very long time. I sampled a special camaraderie on that tour. There may not have been as many so-called 'star' players as on previous Lions missions. But what we did see was 32 totally-committed individuals who for two months at least became friends, all heading in the same direction towards one goal . . . an historic British Lions triumph.

CHAPTER TEN

Collapse of a Dream

SOON after the Lions returned from Australia, and after considerable thought, I rejected a chance to go with the World XV on their somewhat clandestine trip to South Africa. The wheeling and dealing had been going on while we were Down Under because what the Springboks really wanted was for the Lions to go there as a squad. The tour management knew nothing about it, of course, but we were all approached, using certain players as intermediaries. The reaction was mixed; some of the boys wanted to go and some weren't keen on the idea, whilst others objected on principle. The end result was that there was no uniformity and ultimately the Lions venture fell through. However, the South Africans persisted with the concept of a World team under the management of former Lions captain Willie John McBride and a fortnight or so before the trip took place I received a phone call asking me specifically if I would go.

Playing in South Africa was something that really appealed to me and I spent the next couple of days chewing over the prospect. The big stumbling block was my job – and the fact that the Labour-controlled police authority was highly unlikely to approve of the idea. Whilst the RFU tried to keep the venture out of the public eye, they did give it their tacit approval and the South African approach was made within the rules. I received a letter from the South African RFU board at the end of July 1989 inviting me to join the tour squad, and this was followed by a communication from RFU secretary Dudley Wood, who was clearly concerned about reports of illegal payments being made to players should they agree to take part in the tour. Dudley's letter read:

I have been asked to write on behalf of the RFU to all those who have received invitations to play rugby in South Africa, including those who have already declined the invitation, in case there should be a change of heart. In view of the rumours currently circulating, it is important that it is clearly understood that the acceptance of financial inducements or benefits of any kind over and above the allowances specified in the IRFB regulations or described in the letter of invitation would inevitably result in the loss of amateur status and suspension from Rugby Union football. It would be naive to think that any unauthorised rewards would remain secret. Any ban so imposed would be permanent. I'm sorry to write to you in such uncompromising terms.

I also received a copy of a letter sent by Sports Minister Colin Moynihan to the then RFU president Sandy Sanders emphasising that the government was fully committed to the Gleneagles Agreement, under whose terms their policy was to discourage sporting contacts with both teams and individuals from South Africa. The Minister added:

For this reason and because of the possible implications on other sportsmen and women I would wish to discourage rugby players from going to South Africa. It is for the RFU as the governing body and the players as individuals to decide whether or not to accept government advice but I thought I should reiterate our position both to you and the players who receive invitations.

In the end I decided it was just not worth the aggravation of asking for time off work for a trip that could even have cost me my job. As things developed, the tour degenerated into an underhand sort of affair, with players turning up sneakily at Heathrow and slipping out of the country amidst unsubstantiated rumours of large cash payments. Much as I would have liked to have toured in South Africa, that is not the way I would have wanted to do it.

The build-up to the 1990 Five Nations season comprised a warm-up game against Fiji at Twickenham and then, in the New Year, a week-long training camp in Lanzarote. My most vivid memory of the match against the Fijians early in November 1989 is of Paul Ackford tugging at my sleeve for the umpteenth time. 'What are the lineout calls, what are the lineout calls?' he asked yet again, still groggy from the punch that had KO'd him some time before. Reluctantly I repeated the calls and once more Ackers trotted away happily – his legs no longer quite as rickety as Bambi's, but his head still considerably lighter.

He had come off second best, as he invariably did when fists were flying, after taking a swing at Fijian prop Mosese Taga. Paul's swipe probably inflicted more pain on his own hand – because it had no effect whatsoever on Taga. Then came the sequel; as Ackers was running away from a lineout, Taga smacked him from behind and out went the inspector's lights. For the rest of the game my second-row partner was a real pain in the butt, not only to me but most of the other lads too. It's not the easiest of jobs to retain your concentration when someone keeps sidling up and asking the same question he's fired at you half-a-dozen times before.

At least we were spared a repeat of that behaviour a year later, when precisely the same thing happened to Ackers against the touring Argentinians. This time it stemmed from the grilling Jeff Probyn was giving to Frederico Mendez. The Argie prop was big, strong and very capable for a youngster, but he just couldn't cope with Jeff's unorthodox scrummaging. So when he found himself on the floor, he squeezed Jeff's most prized assets and Probes, as any man would do in similar circumstances, stamped on him to escape the agony. Mendez promptly jumped to his feet and took it out on the nearest Englishman . . . who happened to be Ackford.

Once again old Glassjaw's lights went straight out. He was totally pole-axed, in another world. I took a look at him lying there on the deck, his eyes rolling in the back of his head, and removed his gumshield before leaving physio Kevin Murphy to do the rest. Mendez was sent off, as he had to be – and poor Ackers took no further part in the game either. In fact, he was still not right at the after-match dinner in the Rose Room that evening.

As well as the Glassjaw tag, Paul also inherited a second title – Richard Dunn, after the heavyweight boxer who used to spend more time on the canvas than on his feet. On this occasion our still-groggy team-mate received little sympathy as his unfeeling team-mates threw in the towel . . . showering him with a barrage of large white serviettes as he sat at the table, totally baffled by our behaviour.

Apart from the Ackford saga, my main distraction during that game against Fiji was the imminent prospect of becoming a father for the first time. Sharon had already gone the full term and I spent as much time phoning her from Twickenham as I did playing! I rang home before I went into the changing-room, put in another call just before we went on to the pitch, and dashed straight off at the end to make sure everything was all right.

The game itself presented no major problems until frustration caught up with the Fijians, who were getting nowhere in the battle up front and consequently had little opportunity to display their running skills. At the other end Rory Underwood was running in try after try and finally centre Noa Nadruku and Rory's opposite number Tevita Vonolagi lost their heads completely and were sent off by referee Brian Stirling for wild tackles. One of the tackles was so high that Jerry Guscott almost lost his head . . . literally!

Rory finished up equalling England's all-time record of five tries in an international. But I didn't stay to celebrate our 58–23 victory. The RFU had a couple of motor-cycle outriders waiting to escort my car out of Twickenham and through the crowds immediately after the game. With my father and uncle for company, we drove straight back up the M1 to await the imminent arrival. However, using her female prerogative, our baby daughter chose not to arrive on time and made her grand entrance all of ten days late.

Dad was there looking on proudly at Blackpool Victoria Hospital maternity unit when Sophie Helen was born at a healthy weight of nine pounds on 14 November 1989. She was our first child after nine years of marriage – and arrived, of course, in open defiance of strict instructions that any children must be born out of the rugby season!

It was the usual bad timing, just like our wedding day back in 1980, when most of the Hoppers players had to come on to the reception later in the evening because the ceremony clashed with a Merit Table game against Wakefield. And to make matters worse we had a Police Cup game during the week so Sharon and I didn't even have a honeymoon!

Because of injury problems I had dropped out of the British Lions side which beat France under floodlights in Paris in October 1989 in a match to celebrate the bi-centenary of the French Revolution. But I did have the privilege of playing for the Barbarians against New Zealand at Twickenham the following month.

The All Blacks had been on a short tour including Tests against Ireland and Wales, which they won easily. We fielded a fairly strong Baa-Baas side, and although we lost the game 21–10 I found it of enormous benefit in building back towards Championship fitness. Preparations complete, it was on into the 1990 Five Nations campaign – and a season that was to end in high drama with an historic winner-take-all showdown between ourselves and the Scots at Murrayfield.

But first we flew out to Lanzarote for the training camp that was becoming customary practice in our build-up to the Championship. We had switched a year earlier from our previous base in the Algarve, but the purpose of the trip was still the same. It reintroduced the boys to the squad environment after Christmas, focused minds on the job in hand and enabled us to finalise our Five Nations preparations. The Club La Santa complex caters mainly for top track and field athletes from all over the world and we found ourselves training in the company of big-name stars like Steve Ovett and Merlene Ottey. As they went through their drills on the running track, we would go through our schedule on the grassed area in the centre of the stadium – and what a contrast the two forms of preparation were!

We must have looked a real rag-bag outfit to the finely-tuned, immaculately turned-out track stars. If anyone has ever seen an England rugby squad in training they will know what I mean. While we are all issued with identical training kit at the start of each season, the players tend to take the individual approach and wear a real hotch-potch of different track-suit bottoms, jerseys and tee-shirts – not to mention the odd player carrying his boots in a Tesco's bag! We managed to look reasonably tidy during the early part of the week, but the build-up of blood, sweat, grass stains and dirt over the next few days soon put paid to that. Those pristine athletes, whose whole purpose is to cushion themselves from the slightest injury, must have cringed as they watched us go through our rucking, mauling and tackle-bag drills. And I dread to think what they thought of the heated exchanges that took place as feelings spilled over in the ferocious 4 × 20-minute game that rounded off the week.

Some of the boys found the scenery considerably more interesting than the squad work – and I'm not referring to the island landscape but the glamorous contours of Merlene Ottey. They just sat and watched, open-mouthed, as the Jamaican sprint queen went through her training drills in the figure-hugging lime-green body stocking that has become her hallmark. When a couple of members of our front-row fraternity discovered they were staying in the next apartment to Merlene, the writing was on the wall for the green goddess. We were having a drink at the bar late one evening with some American and Swedish field athletes when the two forwards, who shall remain nameless, disappeared. We thought no more of their absence until they suddenly reappeared at the top of the winding staircase and treated us to a hilarious camp fashion show as they descended to the bar area. One of the pranksters had removed his own clothes and somehow squeezed his bulky body into Merlene's lime-green leotard . . . while the other had shoe-horned himself into a tiny bra and pants set also borrowed from Miss Ottey's washing line! Poor Merlene is probably wondering to this day how that minuscule body-stocking and bikini came to stretch to the size of a parachute by the time she removed them from the line the following morning. Needless to say, we never saw her in lime green again – otherwise the wind resistance caused by the gusset dragging along the ground would probably have trebled her sprint times!

That incident provided a little light-hearted relief as we prepared for the crucial campaign just ahead. We had learnt a lot from the shambles in Cardiff the previous year, when we had let ourselves down badly at the final hurdle. This time we went into the Championship doubly determined that there was going to be no repeat of our 1989 mistake. Apart from the fact that we were fitter than ever before, we had also developed a ruthless streak – as the Romanians and Fijians had discovered to their cost.

After an abysmal opening 40 minutes, we got just the start we wanted with a 23–0 win over Ireland at Twickenham. Ackers and I began so badly against a typically disruptive Irish lineout unit that we were completely wiped out in the first half. Then we got it together and in the last 20 minutes, as the Irish tired, we turned the screw. Willie Anderson, Neil Francis and Co. just couldn't live with our superior fitness and we emphasised our superiority with three tries in the last eight minutes.

Despite the victory, things were far from rosy in the lineout department. Without winning that much ball themselves, the streetwise Irish combination had closed us down extremely effectively and caused us major problems on our own ball. The failure to dominate the first half was largely down to Paul and myself and the message was clear. We had a lot of work to do before taking on the French.

By the time we finished training at the Racing Club in Paris the day before the game, we were ready for any eventuality. It was a beautiful spring day as we moved on to take a look at the Parc des Princes after lunch . . . but how the weather changed 24 hours later! The warm sunshine had given way to a gale so ferocious that it virtually ripped our jackets off when we went out for our traditional pre-match pitch inspection. Yet despite the near-impossible wind and Brian Moore having to hold the ball steady to prevent it blowing over, Simon Hodgkinson booted us to a memorable win with one of the finest place-kicking displays I have seen. French coach Jacques Fouroux also played right into our hands by picking the wrong team. I have often been mystified by some of France's selections and in recent years they seem to

Winters on the rampage against the United States in the 1987 World Cup

Gareth Chilcott does his penguin impersonation at Hamilton Island, August 1987

Putting on the smile, Fiji-style, with Paul Rendall, Gary Pearce, Bryan Barley, Jeff Probyn and local ladies

The Lions of England take over Sydney Harbour. From left to right: Jerry Guscott, Rob Andrew, Dean Richards, myself, Paul Ackford, Mike Teague and, in front, Brian Moore and Rory Underwood

Wet, Wet, Wet . . . a rapid Lions attack on the white-water rafting course in Cairns

Allo, Allo, Allo . . . Paul Ackford, Dean Richards and yours truly on the beat at England's training camp in Portugal

Caught on the Hop . . . the Preston Grasshoppers 1990–91 line-up. Picture: Lancashire Evening Post

"IT'S ALRIGHT WADE - MR TODD HAS AN APPOINTMENT!"

The Lancashire Evening Post's *Ken Wignall gave me a chuckle with his view of my duties as part of Neil Kinnock's police escort during the 1990 Labour Party Conference*

Bubbling over . . . and we had every reason to celebrate after winning the 1991 Grand Slam. Picture by Russell Cheyne

Now bring on the world! The England squad pictured at Tynley Hall before the 1991 World cup

What a team . . . Sophie and Dad in training for the World Cup

Oui did it! Ackers and me after our quarter-final win in Paris. Picture by Colorsport

A never-to-be-forgotten moment . . . shaking hands with Her Majesty before the World Cup final

No chance for Australia's Troy Coker . . . with a slight assist from my line-out support king, Mike Teague. Picture by Dave Shopland of the Sunday Telegraph

Golden moment for the golden boy . . . my Twickenham try against Wales on my 50th England appearance completes back-to-back Grand Slams. Picture by Roger Parker

have made a habit of shooting themselves in the foot. There's no question that they possess the players to take on anyone – the big problem is picking the right personnel! This time Fouroux opted for an ineffective second-row partnership of Dominic Erbani and Thierry Devergie and for some obscure reason moved their best lock, Olivier Roumat, to No. 8. Mike Teague, back after missing the Ireland game, loved that, whilst Ackers and I were back at our best in the lineout. We led 13–0 at half-time, and the French were never in it as we produced one of the best forward performances I could remember. The backs scored three tries, Hodgy kicked 14 points and we won 26–7 – assisted by the vociferous support of a huge travelling English army.

Although I began the move that led to our first try, I actually missed the score itself . . . because I was wrestling with their captain Laurent Rodriguez! I stole the ball at a French lineout near half-way, and promptly found myself surrounded by several rival forwards, with Rodriguez determined not to let me escape. Heads, fists and feet flew in all directions as I found myself battling it out alone with not a team-mate in sight – and the next thing I knew the boys were trotting back to the middle, celebrating a try! While Rodriguez and I were having our little contretemps, Rob Andrew had cut back down the blindside and chipped into the corner for Rory Underwood to chase through and score. Referee Owen Doyle did absolutely the right thing in allowing play to continue whilst the altercation was going on. I honestly believe that unless a mass brawl breaks out, the best policy in individual confrontations is for officials to ignore the incident and let it blow itself out. No one ever gets hurt in a stand-up fight, so it makes sense to keep the play going.

Up to that point, I had only once been on the winning side against Wales in six attempts; but it was no contest at Twickenham as we completely dominated them in every phase. The Welsh might have been on a downer, but they still had class players in the shape of Paul Thorburn, Mark Ring, Mike Hall, Arthur Emyr and Phil Davies. Yet they simply weren't in it after we knocked the resistance out of them early on with our vastly superior scrummaging.

We took a couple of strikes against the head, then rubbed it in by lifting their front row and shunting them almost over their own line before pinching their ball. All they managed in reply to our four tries and another 18 points from Hodgy was a late score by Davies. The fire of the Dragon had been well and truly doused and ironically that 34–6 trouncing heralded a new era in attitudes. The Welsh have never come near to beating us since, yet until that day they were the nation we most wanted to topple, the side we loved to hate. It was a title the Scots were about to inherit.

Although we missed out on the next round of matches, there was no let-up in our commitment. Three impressive victories, 11 tries and 83 points had put us within 80 minutes of the first English Grand Slam since, with my Hoppers mates, I had watched Bill Beaumont's boys tame the Scots a decade earlier. Now we were on the verge of repeating the feat – and after a much more impressive build-up, too. Ireland, France and Wales had not only been disposed of, they had been destroyed. Whether we took them on up front, ran at them through the backs or relied on our goalkicking maestro, the points had rattled up from all directions. We just couldn't go wrong and apart from the opening 40 minutes against the Irish, everything had clicked for us right through the campaign.

As a result, team morale was at an all-time high when we gathered in Richmond on our free Saturday for a special squad weekend, and watched on TV at our hotel as the Scots recorded an unimpressive 13–9 win over Wales in Cardiff. It was a victory that set up the most dramatic finale in Five Nations history. Everything was at stake – Calcutta Cup, Championship, Triple Crown, Grand Slam, the lot. Never before had so much hinged on one game, and in view of our convincing performances and Scotland's more dour successes over the same opponents, we were destined to start strong favourites. I had experienced too many previous setbacks, including one nightmare hammering in Scotland in 1986, and although confident I was wary of taking the Scots for granted. After all, it was only 12 months since we had gone to Cardiff as favourites with the Championship within our grasp and blown it.

Certainly the build-up could not have been better. Scottish fans turned up in their droves to watch our training sessions in Peebles; everyone, it seemed, wanted to get a preview of the great English side who were such hot favourites to sweep the board. They weren't disappointed, either, because our Friday run-out went like a dream. I don't remember one ball being spilt all morning. By the time we arrived at Murrayfield on the big day, we were really buzzing. In retrospect, perhaps some of the boys were buzzing too much – with over-confidence.

Geoff Cooke's preparation had by this time become so professional and finely tuned that he also had a sports psychologist, Dave Collins from St Mary's College in Twickenham, travelling with us throughout that season, and indeed the next one. Dave would observe the players and assess the way individuals coped with the pressures of international rugby, providing each of us with a personalised report and suggestions as to how our mental approach could benefit our game. While Dave was with us that day, certainly neither side needed motivating. Every nation wants to put one over the English – and none more so than the Scots. In one way I suppose it is a back-handed compliment, but they can become so paranoid about it that when the result goes against them you visualise depressed fans committing suicide!

Much has been made of the psychological impact of their gladiatorial march on to the Murrayfield turf behind skipper David Sole. I scarcely noticed them follow us out and while it may have motivated the Scottish team and their supporters, it certainly didn't intimidate or surprise us. With old-stagers like Sole, Finlay Calder, John Jeffrey and Derek White in the side, not to mention the wiles of coach McGeechan, the canny Scots were never short of new tricks to try and psyche the opposition out . . . particularly where the English were concerned.

Sole did, however, have a decisive impact on the field because ultimately I believe his blatant gamesmanship saved the Scottish lightweight pack from being overwhelmed. David had impressed me on the Lions tour with his fierce commitment. He was the complete prop, compact, mobile and a very capable loose head and his premature retirement is a great loss to the game. Having said that, he always had problems when he played against Jeff Probyn, mainly because Jeff is so unorthodox and naturally strong in his upper body. As a result David over the years started resorting to all sorts of tactics like grabbing hold of Jeff's outside leg, a ploy which is not only illegal but dangerous as well.

The Scots made a storming start, as we had expected, hurtling into the rucks like only they can. They put us under so much early pressure that they forced us into errors and with the resulting penalties Craig Chalmers kicked them into a 6–0 lead. Then Jerry Guscott scored a great try and our forwards started to get on top. We knew we had the beating of them in the front five, and as half-time approached began to exert continued pressure near the Scottish line. As we tried to apply the *coup de grace* by rolling them over their own line, Sole reacted by taking the scrum down. Referee David Bishop responded by awarding us another scrum . . . and another . . . and another. We were so convinced we would push them over that at one point we even opted for a scrum rather than a penalty shot at goal.

Sole's gamesmanship should really have been punished by a penalty try, but Mr Bishop was having none of that. Perhaps he thought we weren't shunting them back quickly enough. I was as frustrated as anyone because, being on the same side of the scrum as Sole, I could feel what was going on and how much pressure we were exerting. It was only a matter of time before their resistance broke. Or so we thought. A lot of the much-publicised bad feeling between Probyn and Sole stemmed from that game. Some people say Jeff's scrummaging is so unorthodox it can only be classed as cheating, but if anyone was cheating that day it was the Scottish skipper. He took the risk and he got away with it. In other words, he played the captain's role perfectly.

Mr Bishop must have been aware there was a reason for the scrummage going down; and it most certainly wasn't coming from our side. Why on earth would the attacking pack want to collapse when they are camped on their opponents' line, looking to push them over it? The biggest buzz a front five can get is to shunt the opposition back at the scrummage. It rarely happens in international rugby, and it's something those on the receiving end take as a personal affront. It is also a tremendous psychological blow, and if it had happened at that point, I'm convinced Scottish heads would have dropped and we would have taken the game.

Ironically, as we piled on the pressure up front, Will Carling's lack of specific involvement caused his captaincy to be called into question. There were claims later that pack-leader Brian Moore had been making the decisions for him. The general consensus among the forwards, as voiced by Brian, was that we had the Scots on the rack at that point. We needed to keep them on their line and under pressure and that fact was recognised and accepted by Will.

We found ourselves trailing 9–4 at half-time after Chalmers kicked a third penalty and within minutes of the restart that became 13–4. Mike Teague inexplicably tried to pick the ball up at the base of a scrum on half-way, knocked on – and from the resulting set-piece Tony Stanger won the chase to touch down Gavin Hastings's chip through. When we sat down and dissected the game video at the post-match inquest, Mike was still at a loss as to why he went for a pick-up in that position. There was no move called and nothing on for us at the time so the only logical tactic was for Richard Hill to enable Rob Andrew to kick for position.

We still believed the chances would come if we kept applying pressure; but Scott Hastings produced an incredible last-ditch tackle to prevent Rory from scoring and with Hodgkinson having a rare kicking off-day, the spectre of defeat was looming large. As the minutes ticked away we were pressing under the Scottish posts when I drove into a ruck head first, Scottish style, as if to prove a point. My neck was forced back by the impact . . . and an agonising pain shot across my shoulders, followed by a pins-and-needles sensation down my arm and a loss of feeling. I lay there, convinced I had broken my neck, waiting for Ben Gilfeather and Kevin Murphy to diagnose the worst.

Up in the gods at the back of the West Stand, Sharon rummaged through her handbag for her glasses, thinking at first that it was Paul Ackford who had been pole-axed. When the truth dawned on her and she watched the St John's people race on with a stretcher, she started to get her things together to come down to the dressing-room. After prolonged treatment, the feeling gradually returned and I managed to struggle to my feet. I had never left the field before and there was no way I was going off this time – particularly with us pressing so close to the Scots line and precious little time to go. In any case, the RFU doctor would not have let me continue had he thought I was seriously hurt. Sharon was not impressed as the stretcher was waved away and I prepared to play on. In fact, she was furious . . . and she didn't hide her feelings. It was reported in the Press later that she called me 'a big daft sod' but she insists her expletives were not as polite as that!

In the event, my continued presence made no difference. The Scots held out, we lost 13–7 – and I spent the rest of the weekend nursing a shattered dream, a ricked neck and a raging headache. We had played some tremendous rugby, on the day as well as throughout the season, yet once again we had fallen at the final hurdle. For all our promise, all our style and all our efforts, the cupboard was as bare as ever. Proud Will's Army had been sent homewards tae think again . . .

CHAPTER ELEVEN

A Latin Lesson

THE huge cenotaph outside the Sheraton Hotel in Buenos Aires brought home the reality of a war that had faded in the memories of those not directly involved. Decked out with flowers, this memorial, a tribute to the Argentinians who died in the Falklands conflict, was a stark reminder that we were ambassadors trying to rebuild bridges with a nation who had been our sworn enemies just a few years earlier.

Living so far away, the South Atlantic war had somehow been unreal in England . . . something we read about in the newspapers and watched on the television news. Now we were there in the Argentinian capital and the reality was brought home to us as we watched those same people pay silent homage. Too many servicemen's lives had been lost – on both sides.

We arrived in Argentina for our 1990 summer tour at roughly the same time as Britain's first ambassador since the restoration of diplomatic relations following the Falklands hostilities, and he stated during our visit to the embassy that the England tour actually made his settling-in period immeasurably easier. From the way we were treated generally throughout the trip, you would never have guessed what had gone on less than a decade before. The people were friendly, polite and respectful as we strolled through the city, clearly identifiable from our distinctive England tour gear, taking in the cosmopolitan grandeur of what was for most of us our first meaningful look at Latin America.

The trip from the airport into Buenos Aires had been one of remarkable contrasts. The extremes of poverty and comparative wealth were plainly visible as we passed through slums and shanty towns on the outskirts of the capital into the remarkable beauty of the city itself.

The England party had a somewhat experimental look about it in the wake of our Grand Slam disappointment. Rumour had it that the tour had been conceived by a couple of committee men from the two countries over a gin and tonic at an official IRFB function in the not-too-distant past. Certainly it was a badly-timed tour, coming as it did in July and August instead of the customary time just after the English season. It meant those of us who travelled to Argentina had to remain at peak fitness throughout the summer and had no time to relax before the new season. Consequently, when senior players like Rob Andrew, Rory Underwood, Dean Richards, Mike Teague and Paul Ackford decided they would prefer a rest, they were put under no pressure to travel.

In the event, it proved disastrous to embark on such a challenging venture without so many key figures. Argentina's record on their own patch spoke for itself; they had not lost a Test series at home since 1974 and we discovered in our very first game just how tough the challenge was going to be.

The opening match of any tour is normally a banker victory, but the Banco Nacion players obviously hadn't read the script. I sat in the stand and watched as an inexperienced England side, with four uncapped men in the front five, struggled against a bigger and more battle-hardened unit. The end product was that we were beaten by the remarkable boot of the old maestro as Hugo Porta kicked 21 points in their 29–21 victory.

It was a rude awakening . . . and worse was to follow. Our next game four days later took us inland to Tucuman, and a real eye-opener against the Argentinian provincial champions. They hadn't had an out-of-province referee there for three years because the last one had been bombarded with oranges and other missiles as he left the pitch and then reportedly assaulted by a Tucuman player in the tunnel. It just so happened the ref in question had been the official representative of the Argentine referees' society – and he immediately slapped a ban on his fellow officials going there which stood until our visit.

After the Sheraton in Buenos Aires, our hotel was pretty basic, though not quite as appalling as the changing-rooms at the Tucuman ground, which would scarcely have done justice to council-run public park facilities at home.

As for the game itself, it seemed no one had bothered to tell the 20,000 crowd that the Falklands War had ended eight years earlier. It was always going to be a fruitful evening since all the roads leading to the ground were lined with orange trees and chucking them at the ref and the opposition seemed, apart from rugby, to be the favourite local sport. What we were not prepared for as we ran out under the floodlights was the sight of a Union Jack burning away merrily at the back of the Kop! It didn't really ring true afterwards when it was explained that this gesture was nothing against the English themselves; the supporters burnt every visiting team's flag. A comforting thought!

The crowd turned out to be more hostile than the Tucuman team, who were expected to provide us with one of our toughest games outside the Tests. In the event, Nigel Redman and I creamed their lineout men and although Simon Hodgkinson went off injured, a couple of late penalties by David Pears clinched our first victory of the tour. That 19–14 success was still our only win by the time the first Test came round because we proceeded to lose our next two games, 26–23 against a Buenos Aires Select XV and then when Cuyo scraped a 22–21 win in Mendoza with a try two minutes from time.

While we were in Mendoza, Richard Hill, Dean Ryan, Nigel Redman and I decided we'd like to see more of the country so, hiring a vehicle, we set off up into the Andes as far as the Chilean border. Since the trip was considered of cultural value, we managed to get Geoff Cooke to finance part of it from the tour fund, and it proved to be a fascinating experience. The sting came when we got back, because we were all heavily fined by the team court, presided over by Judge Mark Linnett, for being cultural bores!

When they were not training or playing, most of the boys quite rightly just wanted to relax – be it in a bar, swimming pool, casino or whatever. They were all for having a good time; nothing too energetic or taxing on the mind. People seem to think rugby tours are just one wonderful extended holiday, but in reality there are vast amounts of travelling involved, not to mention the hassle of living out of a suitcase.

When players are not travelling they are invariably training or preparing for a game, so there is really very little time for anything else. So when I found myself with a free afternoon, my idea of relaxation was to get out of town and see a bit of whatever country I was visiting at the time. I remember during the 1988 England tour of Australia jumping on a bus with a few of the other boys and taking a one-and-a-half hour ride from Cairns into the rain forest of Northern Queensland. It wasn't everyone's cup of tea but I for one found it a highly rewarding experience. Richard Hill, who is even more culturally inclined than me, actually organised a trip to Soweto during England's 1984 tour to South Africa . . . and got some awful stick for it, too!

The first Test presented me with a personal landmark; it was my 35th cap and took me past Bill Beaumont's England record for a lock. Although a milestone in my career and quite an honour and achievement to be up there with the big genial Lancastrian, it was merely a statistic for the record books. For the boys at Hoppers, however, it was something for them to shout about in the rivalry between Preston and Fylde and I was sure that back home the opportunity wasn't being squandered. I was more preoccupied with the job in hand since it was essential we beat Argentina convincingly to regain credibility after our nightmare start to the tour.

Our team for the Test showed eight changes from the side which lost at Murrayfield four months earlier, and we fielded four new caps in Jason Leonard, Nigel Heslop, Dean Ryan and David Pears. Packing down on the loose-head side behind Leonard to accommodate Redman, I had an opportunity to see at first hand what an excellent prospect Jason was. The 55,000-capacity Velez Sarsfield soccer stadium was about two-thirds full, but the Argentinian fans had little to shout about as Ryan scored an early debut try and we went on to win 25–12. We had come good when it mattered and the only worrying aspect for me was that I took a knock in the ribs that left me in considerable pain.

With just a week between the Tests, it was touch and go whether I made the second game. X-rays at a Buenos Aires hospital revealed no break or cartilage damage, but the ribs were badly bruised and although I trained with them heavily strapped, I broke down a couple of days before the match. It looked ominous, but then the pain eased off again and I decided that with plenty of padding I could probably get through the 80 minutes.

In the meantime, we moved on to Cordoba for our final provincial fixture . . . a game that was to produce a narrow 15–12 victory and one of the few unsavoury moments of the tour. John Olver, leading the side for the first time, found himself embroiled in a bitter, bad-tempered affair – unable to call on the assistance of the big guns because we were resting in the stand in preparation for the second Test. To make matters worse, one of the Cordoba locks was overdoing the physicals and with no England forward experienced enough to keep him under control, this particular Argie bully was going from strength to strength.

At one point Olver called the local referee aside and threatened to take his team off unless he cracked down on the problem. He didn't and when this big second-row found himself on the ground, captain Olver, forgetting his role as ambassador, momentarily had a brainstorm. Unseen by the referee he took the law into his own hands, and kicked the offending Argentinian – and was lucky to stay on the pitch.

The ground erupted with outraged Argentinian fans leaping to their feet in a storm of Latin fury, screaming abuse and baying for

Olver's blood. It seemed another war was about to start on the terraces. With the management and bench safely down on the touchline, the rest of us in the stand decided unanimously that discretion was the better part of valour and, removing all signs of the red rose, we melted into the crowd. It was perhaps an indication of Olver's popularity on that tour as chief sneak to the players' court judge that, not satisfied with just mingling, the boys actually took up the chant to have the miscreant removed from the pitch forthwith.

Eventually peace was restored and the lock recovered to play on, albeit somewhat groggily. But at least the captain's moment of madness had the desired effect because the Argie troublemaker behaved himself perfectly after that. It was also the signal for Olver to inherit a new nickname . . . Norman Hunter.

Back in Buenos Aires, I refused a pain-killing injection before the Test. I have never been convinced of their value. Basically it would always be at the back of my mind during the game just what additional damage I could be causing to the original injury under the influence of a jab. As it happens, things went reasonably well until the second half and we seemed on course for a 2–0 series win when I took a lineout ball, turned and drove through. As I did so, the Argentinian No. 8 Baeck cracked me with his shoulder in my damaged ribs . . . and down I went in agony.

It was a fair and well-timed tackle and one that was to put me out of the game. I had gone on to the pitch fully aware of the risks. The damage was such I couldn't move, never mind scrummage and I had to go off for the only time in my international career with England leading 10–9. Dave Egerton came off the bench to join Redman in the second row, but the game proceeded to drift away from us, courtesy of the boot of Argentine winger Hernan Vidou. His five penalties cancelled out tries by Hodgkinson and Heslop and our embarrassment was complete as we were beaten 15–13.

A 1–1 series draw and four defeats in a seven-game tour was scarcely a major success story, particularly against a nation of only moderate ability. Yet while the trip must rate as a disaster in terms of results, it did at least produce a number of plus points with the emergence of newcomers such as Leonard, Heslop, Tim Rodber and Ryan as players of genuine England quality.

On reflection, I'm glad I took part in the tour, but it proved of little overall benefit to England other than in helping to bring on the new players. For an old hand like myself, who had toured every summer

since 1987, it would have made more sense to have followed the example
of Rory, Rob, Ackers and Co. – and had a rest. Certainly the visit to
Argentina in no way contributed to the historic Five Nations season that
was to follow.

The sting-in-the-tail came just after we boarded our Pan-Am jet in
Buenos Aires for the flight home to London. 'We would like to welcome
everyone aboard,' announced the American pilot. 'Particularly the very
accomplished British soccer team . . .'

We had a chance to make amends for our failings in Argentina just
three months later when they came to Twickenham with a largely
revamped side under a new coach in Luis Gradin. But first England took
on and beat a world-class Barbarians side (albeit only 18–16) in a match
to celebrate the Baa-Baas' centenary. David Campese, Joe Stanley,
Michael Lynagh, Jean Baptiste Lafond and Nick Farr-Jones were all
there, so was my old lineout rival Steve Cutler.

We were more or less at full strength for that one, and also for the
subsequent Test against Argentina. This time it was no contest as we
took the Argies apart from the first whistle. There was no slow start, as
had happened so often in the past. This time we hit them straight away
and never let up. The final result said it all . . . England 51 Argentina 0.
The rout included seven tries, with Hodgkinson kicking ten out of 11
shots at goal, and we could not possibly have had a better morale booster
for the Championship campaign ahead.

CHAPTER TWELVE

Power and Glory: the 1991 Grand Slam

IT was the first and only time I ever crossed swords with Will Carling but his frustration was perfectly understandable. The skipper and Rob Andrew both saw red when I inadvertently dived over the top to give Wales a kickable penalty in the opening game of the 1991 Five Nations season. Although Paul Thorburn missed the shot at goal, to the great disappointment of the Cardiff crowd, my indiscretion represented to Will and Rob an unforgivable lapse in the on-field discipline we had been trying so diligently to improve.

Both of them made their feelings known in no uncertain terms. Furious that a couple of the 'girls' behind the scrum should bawl me out, I responded in kind. In the hostile cauldron of the Arms Park, hot blood got the better of logic and my thoughts were pretty uncompromising. What did they know about the pressures in the engine room when they spent most of their time standing there watching? Didn't they understand that in the unyielding battle for possession, it was inevitable that individuals would occasionally overstep the mark? I spat out a riposte in words that are unprintable.

Later, a 26–7 victory behind us – along with England's 28-year Cardiff jinx – our little disagreement was set aside as the three of us joked about the incident. It was one of those things that happens out on the park, one of those occasions when the intensity of the situation sparks a momentary explosion. Perhaps Will's action at the end of the game summed it all up best. As the final whistle blew, he made a point of jogging over and with a handshake all was forgotten. To me that spoke volumes for both his attitude and his captaincy.

The Wales game had scarcely lived up to the excitement we had generated in our ill-fated Grand Slam challenge the previous year, but no one was concerned about that. We had become more ruthless in our desperation to make up for the bitter disappointments of 1989 and 1990, and it was of no concern to us if it wasn't pretty to watch. Any change of tactics was not a management decision – the tightening up was a conscious effort by the players themselves, prompted by the knowledge that our forwards had the beating of any side in the world. While we had shown we could play it tight or spin the ball with equal success, we wanted that Grand Slam more than anything . . . particularly with the World Cup just nine months away. For all the expansive style of rugby that we had produced the previous year, we still had nothing to show for our efforts. The simple fact was that it was Grand Slams and Triple Crowns people remembered, not entertainment and style. Our supporters as well as ourselves were hungry for a trophy, however intangible that trophy might be.

We spent the Wednesday night before the Wales game in Gloucester, engaged in a fierce training session against the might of the local club's powerful pack at Kingsholm. One can only assume there is very little evening entertainment in the city, because Gloucester supporters were there in their hordes, cheering on their idols as they battled against us in a sequence of scrummages and lineouts.

They gave us a torrid time, too, and our scrummaging left a lot to be desired as they put us under a considerable amount of pressure. That delighted the Kingsholm faithful and we took a fair old ribbing, local hero Mike Teague included, as the fans bayed for the England management to reselect the team, dropping the chosen eight and promoting the Gloucester pack en bloc to national status.

Ultimately that session made little difference to our domination of the Welsh three days later. Yet, for all the sweetness of that long-awaited victory at the Arms Park, we knew we had to improve if we were to avenge our Murrayfield nightmare in the Calcutta Cup showdown at Twickenham. Although we had four weeks to prepare, bad weather limited us to just one get-together; but we were more than ready for David Sole and Co. when the big showdown finally arrived.

After the Grand Slam disaster of 1990, we wanted the Scots badly. Revenge was the name of the game and all the friendships I had made with their players on the Lions tour and with the Barbarians went by the board as we hit them the way they had piled into us at Murrayfield. There was certainly no love lost, as Gavin Hastings found to his cost in the opening couple of minutes when he took a high ball and found the entire English pack swarming over him.

Basically we did what they had done to us at Murrayfield. We stormed into them from the kick-off, keeping it tight, driving in at them at every opportunity, starving them of possession and pinning them in their own half for long periods. In my time the English front five as a unit had invariably held the upper hand against the Scots in the set-piece; and this time was no different. Paul Ackford and I dominated Chris Gray and Damian Cronin and although Sole's men tried to run what scraps of possession they obtained, on this day they lacked the firepower outside the pack, too.

Even so, the discipline that had been so exemplary the previous season almost proved our undoing. We *knew* how crucial it was not to give away penalties in kickable positions, yet whenever we scored, up would pop Craig Chalmers to slot over three points and keep Scotland in the game.

For all our dominance, we were just 15–12 ahead when Nigel Heslop finally lifted the pressure with the game's only try. Rob Andrew's reaction at the final whistle said it all as he punched the air joyfully and gesticulated towards the dejected Scots. Such bad manners and needling behaviour was totally out of character for a player who is normally so level-headed and sporting. But it showed just how much importance we attached to the result. Our performance may not have been wildly exciting, but we had gained sweet revenge . . . and we were half-way to the Grand Slam.

It had been a clinical exercise, a forward-orientated destruction job which had worn the Scots down. Yet despite our 21–12 victory, there was a scathing video dissection of our performance later, with the emphasis on the disciplinary lapses that had allowed Chalmers to kick his four penalties.

The Triple Crown beckoned as we ran out to face Ireland a couple of weeks later on a miserable day in Dublin. When we shunted the Irish forwards back early on and received a penalty decision for an Irishman straying offside, the omens looked good for us. But Simon Hodgkinson missed the kick . . . and before we knew it Brian Smith had slotted one over to put *them* 3–0 in front.

Fortunately we levelled it with a penalty just before half-time, but it was a day when the conditions were against flowing rugby. We failed to establish lineout superiority, and every time we attacked their defence was simply incredible. At one point we stormed towards their line over and over again in a sustained attack, yet failed to penetrate their line as they knocked us back every time and we actually finished up outside their 22!

Referee Alain Ceccon's over-officiousness added to the problems as both sides tried desperately to find their rhythm. We had a nightmare start to the second half when Simon Geoghegan powered past Rory Underwood's defences, squeezing into the corner to give Ireland a 7–3 lead. Nothing seemed to be going right although we did have one fortunate moment when an enormous gap opened up after Rob had gone blind in defending a five-metre scrum. Had Smith been confident enough to go for that gap we could well have seen a try under the posts and a 13–3 deficit. But instead the Irish outside-half decided to chip over the defence for his wing, unsuccessfully as it turned out, and we escaped with our line intact.

Although Hodgy landed another penalty, we were still a point adrift going into the last quarter. However, unlike the England teams I had been associated with in earlier years, there was no panic. Instead we called on our reserves of character, self-confidence and fitness, and gradually the Irish resistance began to crumble. Finally, with just 10 minutes left, Rory outwitted four Irish defenders to speed in for a try . . . and they folded. Their forwards were virtually out on their feet, totally exhausted, and as the seconds ticked away it was time for our eight to turn the screw. Inevitably the pressure told and Mike Teague added another try in injury time.

The Triple Crown was ours! It had taken me seven seasons, and the 16–7 triumph in Dublin may not have been pretty to watch; but England, my England, had finally won something to end the disappointment and heartache that had haunted us for so many years. Now we faced a repeat of the previous season's finale – a Grand Slam decider against another unbeaten side. Only this time it was France, not Scotland, who stood between us and the biggest prize in northern hemisphere rugby.

There was also one other important difference . . . we were playing in front of our own fans at Twickenham. However, it was just as formidable a challenge against a team which had totally destroyed the Welsh in Paris. We analysed a video of France's 36–3 demolition job, and what we saw only served as a warning. Albeit against inferior opposition, the French were dominant in all aspects of the game. This was uninhibited Gallic rugby back to its very best.

We concentrated on a low-key approach to the big match. It was not easy, but it was important to prepare as thoroughly as possible and treat it as just another game, avoiding the hype that would obviously surround the build-up. We already had the Triple Crown, and it was a measure of how far we had come that two years earlier we would happily have settled for that. Now it was merely a prelude to the one that really mattered – the Grand Slam that had eluded us so frustratingly 12 months earlier.

The night before the game, I received a hastily-written note from Will Carling in my room at the Petersham team hotel. No doubt 14 others received similar messages but mine read:

> Wade, With over 40 caps there's bugger-all I can say but you know how important you are to us tomorrow. You've carried us through three games – let's kill these buggers off in the fourth. Make sure you get to run with the ball too and hurt these idiots in every tackle. This is our biggest game so let's show everyone how powerful we are. Good luck mate. Will.

Despite the massive importance of the match, the following morning was little different to any home international build-up. Each player has his own way of preparing, and over the years my routine before Twickenham games had rarely changed. I ordered tea in bed for 8 a.m., settled down to read the newspapers, and around nine ambled down for breakfast in the team room. As usual I was the first player there, joining other early birds like Kevin Murphy, Ben Gilfeather and Roger Uttley for what was to be my only meal until we reached the Hilton Hotel for the Grand Slam dinner later that evening.

During the morning the Petersham would provide pre-match food at specific times ordered individually by players the previous evening. Some had requested pasta while Brian Moore had asked for his regular appetiser – a plate of mashed potatoes. But for me a breakfast of grapefruit, scrambled egg on toast, banana, honey and tea was more than enough to see me through the day.

Around 10 o'clock Paul Ackford and I took our customary 20-minute stroll down Richmond Hill and along the banks of the Thames, then it was back to the Petersham – which overlooks the river – for coffee and to clean my boots and pack my bags. At 11 the forwards trooped into Dean Richards's room for our team meeting, while the backs had their own separate get-together. We spent 20 minutes going over specifics like lineout and scrummage calls and back-row moves. Then, as the players slumped around in an array of casual attire, Roger followed up a general chat with his own brief say about the game plan.

Back in my room, I checked that my boots, shinpads, gumshield and other essentials were in my kit-bag, along with training shoes for the pre-match workout on the scrummaging machine in the Twickenham changing-room. After showering and changing into blazer and greys it was downstairs for the final team meeting in the team room. The hotel had by now taken on an air of strange tranquillity. There was no laughing and joking; the pranks of the previous day had been left behind. It was deadly serious now . . . the only thing that mattered was concentrating totally and looking inwards to one's own individual build-up.

Little was said at the meeting, but this was the time when I was at my most nervous. A few butterflies, a little trepidation, but nothing like as bad as in the early part of my international career. Snacks, sandwiches and soup were there for the people who wanted them, but the greatest demand throughout the morning had been for bananas, which the boys devoured in copious amounts.

An hour-and-a-half before kick-off it was on to the coach and, escorted by our customary police motor-cycle escort, through the narrow streets of Richmond and Twickenham to the stadium, switching to the wrong side of the road on occasion to avoid the traffic bottlenecks. For as long as I can remember I have always sat in the right-hand seat at the very back. It's not a superstition, just something I have always done.

We were cheered enthusiastically by the crowds outside as we neared the stadium, then it was off the coach to beat a narrow snaking path through hordes of back-slapping well-wishers to the dressing-room. The autograph hunters were there, too, and although I hate refusing to sign and disappointing people, especially the youngsters, this was not the time for it. I explained that we would happily sign every last one of them after the game. But only one thing mattered now . . .

The opponent who particularly concerned us was Serge Blanco. He may have been playing his final Five Nations game, but we regarded the French captain's match-winning brilliance as potentially the biggest threat of all. It was clear his attacking menace had to be countered, so one of the key aspects of our battle plan was to pressurise him at every opportunity and give him no scope to attack – from anywhere on the field. Ten minutes into the game Blanco had ripped that blueprint to shreds.

Obviously concerned about our forward strength, the French

tactics were patently clear right from the start; they were going to run the ball at every opportunity, regardless of where they were. That played straight into our hands after only three minutes when Pierre Berbizier tried to run a drop-out. One of his team-mates fumbled, Peter Winterbottom picked up and drove back at them and they conceded a penalty which Simon Hodgkinson accepted gratefully.

It was a dream start for us, 3–0 ahead in no time and shortly afterwards Hodgy had a chance to make it 6–0 when a Frenchman was caught offside. But this time he missed – and it could not have proved costlier. Berbizier collected the ball behind his own line, Blanco looped behind him and off went the French backs on an amazing length-of-the-field move to score one of the greatest tries Twickenham will ever witness.

We had seen some stunning rugby from the French in the past but this was something special. With our cover flooding across, Philippe Sella and Didier Camberabero worked a huge scissors on the right before Camberabero raced away, and when he cross-kicked into the middle, Philippe Saint Andre picked up and galloped in under the posts. Later, reliving the game on video, we had to applaud the sheer brilliance of the try. But we certainly didn't appreciate it that much at the time!

Obviously it came as quite a blow from an English point of view, but it was scored far too early in the game for us to be worried. What was of more concern to me personally was my own ineffectiveness in the lineout, where Abdel Benazzi's presence behind my opposite number Olivier Roumat caused me no end of problems. I didn't know Benazzi, but he had clearly been brought in to keep me quiet and with the aid of a fair bit of bumping and barging he succeeded. In fact I scarcely won a lineout all day and had more problems in that game than any other international I can remember.

However, such was the relationship between myself and Paul Ackford that you could guarantee if one of us had an off-day the other would hit peak form. And that's exactly how it worked out as Ackers shrugged off the challenge of a very ordinary newcomer in Michel Tachdjian and played a blinder.

My lineout woes apart, we gave the French pack a good hiding up front, starving them of possession in another highly impressive pack performance. With such a powerful platform, Hodgy's boot gradually eased us into the lead, and in the highly-charged atmosphere, French indiscipline began to show itself as it has done so often in recent years.

At one point we were driving through and I ended up on the floor close to the West Stand touchline with Jason Leonard on top of me. I was pinned down and powerless to do anything as French prop Pascal Ondarts punched Jason, but amazingly referee Les Peard missed the blow – and so did touch-judge Clive Norling. I was puzzled about what Norling was doing, since he was standing only a matter of a yard away from the incident and must have seen the punch. 'Open your eyes,' I bawled at him, the inference being that instead of watching the game he was too busy preening himself and getting his best side on camera. I was promptly told in no uncertain terms where to stick my suggestion.

Norling had a second go at me moments later as we awaited a restart at half-way, but at least I knew exactly where I stood with him. The big Welshman is to my mind the best referee the game has produced in recent years, and like most international players I have always had a great deal of respect for him. He was never one for taking any messing, and the verbals he aimed in my direction were typical of his approach.

It had been a bit of gamesmanship on my part, maybe, but it backfired. Players who appeal to officials on the field usually get short shrift, as I did that day, while Ondarts smiled knowingly and got on with the game. The penalty may have eluded us on that occasion but the indiscipline of Ondarts' team-mate Xavier Blond in the closing stages possibly cost France the match. We were clinging to an 18–13 lead when flanker Blond lost his rag after being penalised for going over the top – and grabbed referee Peard by his shirt. He should have known better than to manhandle an official, particularly when the referee in question is a policeman! Peard promptly moved the penalty 10 yards nearer the French line, turning a difficult goal attempt into a relatively easy one, and Simon kicked it to extend our lead to eight points. Ironically for France, Franck Mesnel scored a late try which Camberabero converted to reduce our final victory margin to just 21–19, so who knows how much Blond's moment of madness really cost them?

The last few frenetic minutes seemed endless, but desperate defence gave way to an enormous sense of relief and unmitigated joy as the final whistle sounded. We'd done it! We had finally emulated Bill Beaumont's men a decade earlier and carved our own little slice of history. It was a case of third time lucky after those devastating setbacks in 1989 and 1990. And how fitting that the culmination of years of hard work should come in front of our own delirious supporters after such an exhilarating game. The euphoria in the changing-rooms was unimaginable . . . and the champagne did not stop flowing all night.

Later in the evening, the team dinner at the Hilton over, Sharon and I headed for a further celebration at a nearby wine bar, courtesy of Micky Skinner's mate Ian Botham. The scenes as we left the hotel resembled an Oscar night in Hollywood as a barrage of Press flashlights lit up the path to our taxi. The paparazzi were still snapping away and dazzling us as we drove off into the night; only by now the cameras were blazing away against the windows of the taxi.

I had never met Botham before, but it was easy to understand why he and Skins got on so well together. How does the saying go . . . birds of a feather? Basically they were a couple of larger-than-life characters out for a good time. We had a pretty fair idea there was going to be some fun and games when the ice-buckets started filling up, so Sharon and I decided to get out while the going was good. And just as well too because Beefy and Skins were obviously lining up a massive bucketing session – and heaven help anyone who got in the way!

In the cold, slightly hazy light of the following day we all came down to earth with a bump. The Sunday papers were of course full of our glorious victory but that was as far as it went. We had won the elusive Grand Slam in front of a sell-out Twickenham crowd and captured the hearts and imagination of the TV sporting public, not just at home but around the world, with an all-too-rare English success.

Some time later, at the Middlesex Sevens, each England player was presented by the Rugby Football Union with an inscribed glass tankard etched with his profile. Yet at the time of winning the 1991 Grand Slam our achievement was marked by neither a trophy nor individual presentations. On the Sunday we just went home . . . and it was back to work on Monday morning.

Make and Break Time

ENGLAND'S summer tour to Australia was to be our last real chance to prepare for the World Cup before the all-important opening match against the holders, New Zealand, on 3 October. We knew that on returning home we would face a series of warm-up games against the USSR, Gloucester and an England Students XV, but the players were under no illusions about those fixtures. They were just the management's way of keeping the squad ticking over prior to the tournament itself and indeed were to present the players with motivation problems. By the time the Soviet game came round in September, Geoff Cooke had gathered together a team of regional coaches who sat in the stand at Twickenham and were each given an individual player to spotlight. My lacklustre performance that day led my personal assessor to report that on that form I wasn't worth my place in the side!

We flew out to Sydney in July against a backdrop of Press speculation that the tour was badly timed and created extra pressure just when the players needed a rest before the World Cup. That was certainly not my way of thinking. Apart from 1986, when the Lions trip to South Africa was called off, I had never known a summer without touring – and for my part it was the ideal way of keeping at the peak of fitness.

In touring terms, Australia had almost become my second home. Counting the 1989 Lions trip, it was my fourth visit in five years and although this particular tour comprised only seven matches, it was highly significant in gauging where we stood in relation to the southern hemisphere in our World Cup preparations. I was also hoping it would be more productive than my previous England tours because, with the exception of the drawn series in Argentina the previous year, we had invariably finished on the receiving end.

The only pressure on me touring that year arose from family considerations and the fact that I was spending more time away from

Sharon and 20-month-old Sophie. It was a situation Sharon had grown accustomed to over the years but Sophie, despite her tender age, was already beginning to question where her Daddy was. To add to it all, halfway through the tour Sharon broke the news to me that she was expecting our second child.

Dick Best, who was being groomed as Roger Uttley's successor after the World Cup, was wisely included in the tour party to give him the feel of the job and enable him to get to know the players better. He was particularly careful not to tread on anyone's toes, but still took some unmerciful ribbing in his somewhat superfluous role as assistant coach. The job gave him sole charge of all the equipment and kit required for the month-long tour, and the boys quickly dubbed him 'Baggage'. But to his credit he took the stick in good part.

After a few days' acclimatisation we could not have had a more difficult start, being thrown straight in against New South Wales, one of the best provincial sides in the world. Lions apart, I had never been on the winning side against them, and this time they were really buzzing after thrashing Wales by an unbelievable margin of 71–8 just a week earlier.

Any thoughts they had entertained of a second northern hemisphere side lying down and accepting the inevitable were quickly dispelled. Instead we went out and gave a grilling to their forwards, the majority of whom would form the Australian World Cup pack. It was as good an overall performance as we could have hoped for, yet it was not quite good enough. We eventually lost 21–19 although we might well have won had Rob Andrew's late dropped-goal attempt not struck the crossbar.

There was certainly no despondency about our narrow defeat. In fact we were happy in the knowledge that we had played well but still had room for improvement. Certainly our morale and hopes were as high as ever, in total contrast to the internal bickering that was going on among the warring Welsh elsewhere in Australia.

The midweek boys managed to get the victory wagon rolling with a 26–9 win over the Victoria President's XV in Melbourne, only for the good work to be ruined by defeat against Queensland in a match which was effectively to end my tour.

I found myself in opposition for the first time to John Eales, the 21-year-old art student the Aussies were all talking about. I introduced myself early on when, following a drop-out, he found himself beneath the entire England pack. I rubbed his face in the dirt as a good-natured

way of saying hello . . . and followed up with a couple of words of
welcome in his ear.

But my respect quickly grew for the young man, who has since
taken over Steve Cutler's role as Australia's main lineout specialist. Eales
is one of the new-style second rows, less bulky than the heavyweights of
old, remarkably athletic and also at home at No. 8. Whilst he lacks the
upper-body strength of some players, he possesses all the attributes of an
outstanding lock: he jumps effectively, is very mobile, has great hands,
defends well and is good in the tackle. He also has a sense of humour as
I discovered when he came into our dressing-room after the game and,
echoing my earlier comment at the bottom of the ruck, asked: 'Do you
mind changing shirts with an arty-farty student?'

At this point I was nursing an injured hand received towards the
end of the game when we were defending our own line. As the
Queenslanders drove into a ruck, back-row man Sam Scott-Young went
over the top, raking an English player lying on the deck. The offence
was not seen by the referee and in the heat of the moment I stupidly
sought retribution by taking a swing at Scott-Young. It was an instant
reaction and a loss of self-control . . . and I paid for it because he ducked
and I caught him on the top of the head. Then, to add insult to injury,
the cheeky Aussie looked up and smiled at me!

I knew I had done myself some damage and a few minutes later I
called Kevin Murphy on to take a look at my injured right hand. Smurf
took the precaution of strapping it up, but although I managed to
complete the game, my momentary indiscretion was to prove costly.
How much difference my injury made is open to conjecture, but it
certainly inhibited me for the last 20 minutes. And we went on to lose
the game 21–14, our second defeat in three matches.

The problem was also of great concern to England team doctor Ben
Gilfeather because he bundled me straight into a taxi and sent me off to
a local private hospital for an X-ray which revealed the worst. I had
broken a bone in the back of my right hand.

Sick that my immediate England future had been thrown into
jeopardy, I prepared for the worst. Had the hospital decided to plaster
my damaged hand up, I would have been on the next plane back to
England and a replacement flown out, my tour over less than a fortnight
after it began. The Aussie doctor, a rugby enthusiast who had dashed
down from his home after watching the game on TV, decided instead on
a less dramatic course of action; he strapped up the injury in the hope

that I might yet salvage some action in the final game of the tour . . . the Test against Australia a fortnight later.

It quickly became clear I had no chance of playing in our next three matches against Fiji B, Fiji and the Emerging Wallabies. But, bolstered by the doctor's confidence that I could very well make the Sydney Test, I rejoined the party preparing to fly out to Fiji. It was always going to be a 50–50 battle for me, but Geoff Cooke and Roger Uttley felt there was sufficient hope to justify keeping me on the tour; and sure enough the pain and bruising began to decrease by the day. During that period I spent a great deal of time working on a fitness programme with Dick Best. It incorporated so many sit-ups that after joining in, Dick complained to Ben Gilfeather that the muscles were exploding through the wall of his stomach!

By the time we returned to Australia after the two-game mini-tour of Fiji, I was so keen to make the big one that I threw myself into the thick of the scrummaging and contact work more enthusiastically than ever. The hand was still not right but I desperately wanted to play and declared myself ready to do so. Ultimately, however, the decision was made for me because Geoff and Roger, advised by Ben, decided it was too much of a risk.

At the time I was bitterly disappointed but in retrospect it was the right decision. There were scarcely two months to go before the start of the World Cup and, strapping or not, it would have been silly to play with my hand anything but 100 per cent. Another knock at that stage could have had disastrous consequences.

The trip to Fiji provided arguably the worst England tour performance I have been associated with – a shambolic defeat by their B team. The omens seemed good when we arrived on the main island of Viti Levu, to be greeted by the ever-welcoming natives with garlands of flowers before moving on to our idyllic beachside hotel.

I concentrated on keeping in peak condition in preparation for my hoped-for return against Australia, but it was a painful experience to watch the carnival of errors that cost us the Fiji B game at Lautoka. In scorching heat, a largely inexperienced England team let a 13–3 lead slip and finished up losing 27–13 against moderate opposition. It was a disgraceful performance and the only excuse was that we had so many injuries that Simon Hodgkinson finished the game as a none-too-confident outside-half!

The result was totally unexpected and it sent the entire Fijian Islands wild with delight. It was also our third defeat in four tour games

. . . and suddenly the Grand Slam we had achieved just a few months earlier seemed like a distant memory.

A group of us decided to get away from it all by taking a trip around the islands, so Richard Hill, Nigel Redman, Jeff Probyn and myself hired a boat and a guide – and off we went. The Fijian archipelago consists of 300 islands and it seemed that all of them (or at least the 100 or so populated ones) had their own team! Those islands with minimal population would send their players across to play for the next island, and it seemed that absolutely everybody was crazy about the game.

After a glorious afternoon swimming and snorkelling around the numerous coral reefs we decided, typically of Englishmen abroad, that we wanted a cup of tea. Our guide obligingly dropped us off on the beach of another island, where rugby-mad staff from the local hotel, realising we were members of the England team, converged on us. In return for signing autographs and posing for photos with them, we spent the next couple of hours being treated like kings. And after they had served us a high tea of cakes, biscuits, sticky buns, tea and coffee we were escorted down to the beach and waved off enthusiastically as our boat took us back to our base.

The reality of our mission was never far away, however, and we knew that if we were going to salvage anything from what was becoming a nightmare tour in terms of results, we *had* to win the Test against Fiji. Unlike our visit in 1988, when we crossed the island rather unglamorously by charabanc, this time we flew from Nandi to the capital Suva, where Paul Ackford delivered another cutting blow to the selectors. Just 24 hours before the game he cried off with an ankle injury, leaving Redman and Martin Bayfield to team up in a new international second-row partnership. It was the only time Ackers and I were ever sidelined at the same time in a Test match and Paul predictably took some stick for it. In fact, the boys insisted he was pulling out because after so many big games together our umbilical cord had been cut!

It was a strange experience sitting there alongside him in the stand watching a game in which we should both have been playing. And it developed into nailbiting stuff as the Fijian pack, encouraged by a massive partisan crowd, threatened to take control. When Waisale Serevi dropped a goal to make it 12–12 it was anybody's game; and up in the stands we sat, heads in hands, thinking 'Here we go again'. But despite dominating the play for fully 20 minutes, Fiji's inexperience at top level became all too evident. Instead of playing to their strengths they developed dropped-goal fever and started trying to pop them over from everywhere . . . including one prodigious attempt by the fullback from all of 60 yards! There was no such panic from our boys, however, and we coolly took control in the last 15 minutes, stretching away to win 28–12 after Rob Andrew had scored his first try for England . . . in his 37th game! Suddenly the tour was very much alive and we had everything to play for. As ever, the Tests were the games that really mattered and in that area we were half way to a clean sweep.

Back in Australia, the Wallabies warmed up for the big one by caning the increasingly fragmented Welsh 63–6, their biggest-ever Test defeat. We didn't read too much into that result as we prepared for our own bite at the Aussies a week later; and in any case the immediate task was to deal with a powerful Emerging Wallabies side at Gosford, roughly an hour's bus ride from our base at the Pacific Hotel in Manly. The title 'Emerging' Wallabies was hardly apt, since the team was anything but a squad of up-and-coming youngsters as the name might suggest. This particular side was packed with quality players, several of whom had Test experience, yet the boys handled them in style. The 36–3 victory was our best performance of the tour and the perfect morale-booster for the clash with Australia at Sydney Football Stadium.

In my continued absence the Test match plunged Martin Bayfield, who had made an impressive international debut against the Fijians, into direct confrontation with the equally inexperienced Eales. With both men playing only their second Test, I impressed on Martin before the game how important it was for him to dictate the battle on his own terms. In the event the setting, the capacity crowd and the opposition all combined to overawe him somewhat and it was Eales, playing in front of his own support, who gained the upper hand. It was a lesson that would prove invaluable to Martin over the next 12 months.

I took my seat in the stand and watched the agony unfold as the Wallabies back row, inspired by an incredible performance from No. 8 Tim Gavin, gave us a good going over and caught us with a couple of sucker punches into the bargain. Gavin, two-try Willie Ofahengaue and the tough and abrasive Simon Poidevin were a revelation and we had no answer as they stormed to a 40–15 victory. As Roger Uttley admitted, they were a yard faster than us, quicker thinking, bigger and stronger and it showed us exactly where we stood.

There were, however, some bright spots despite a try count of 5–1 in Australia's favour and a scoreline just two points short of our record defeat. We had applied a considerable amount of pressure at times during the game and made some decisive breaks, only to suffer time and again when the final pass failed to go to hand. Having said that, I had to agree with their skipper Nick Farr-Jones's assessment that it was one of the best Aussie performances that he had been involved in. I had never seen the Wallabies play better – and it set a few alarm bells ringing as to what we could expect in two months' time.

The big consolation was that we now knew exactly what was ahead if we had to play the Aussies in the World Cup . . . and we had just a few weeks to find the antidote.

CHAPTER FOURTEEN

The Changing Face of Rugby

I CAN understand the International Board wanting to speed up the game with their new laws on the lineout and rucking and mauling, but from my point of view as a lineout forward, they are taking the emphasis away from an integral part of the game.

By doubling the space between the two sets of forwards to a full metre, the IB's intention seems to be to cut out the confrontation which I think is an essential ingredient of lineout play. If everyone stuck rigidly to the rules, that would mean jumping straight up and down and winning your own ball every time. In short, it would reduce the lineout to a simple, non-competitive means of restarting play. If that is the idea, they might as well use soccer tactics – and allow the side awarded the throw-in to chuck the ball anywhere they like!

There is no finer sight than someone getting a clear jump and soaring like Rudolf Nureyev to take a clean two-handed catch; but too much of a good thing can also make the exercise sterile and boring. The lineout is more than that and for me the most challenging part is the physical confrontation with my opposite number – and trying to come out on top. Take that away and you take away the most exciting aspect of the job, for player and spectator alike.

It has always been accepted practice for lineout forwards to step into the existing half-metre between the teams, and I cannot see it being workable to stop players jumping into that gap and across the line. It is something we all practise in training and I believe that will continue to be the case. I cannot see the new rule eradicating the ploy since it gives lineout men space to play with and makes it more likely the slight taps will come back on your side.

As I have learnt since coming on to the international scene, the lineout is a lot more technical than many people think, with the understanding between the main jumpers, the hookers throwing in and the support players worked out to a fine art. That's why losing Mike Teague in the first minute was such a big blow in the Five Nations decider in Cardiff in 1989. Basically we work as a team, with the two jumpers assisted by three support players (in my case the flanker behind and prop in front of me) and of course the hooker throwing in. The key to successful ball-winning is the team working in unison, minds focused on the job in hand and timing geared to perfection.

In Paul Rendall, England had a prop whose lineout support work was the best in the business, as Paul Ackford will readily testify. Ackers was no slouch at the front of the line, but that so-called standing jump of his was not entirely what it appeared to be. The support play and protection provided by Jeff Probyn, Rendall and later Jason Leonard was the thing that kept him at the top of his jump. It was very much down to the hard work of players like them, and of course Teague, that people like Ackers and myself stayed in the spotlight.

It wasn't only their support play, either, because much of their work entailed preventing your opposite number from interfering with you. To take it to the strict letter of the law, it is illegal. But tactics like supporting and blocking your opposite number are part and parcel of Test rugby – and everybody does it. There is more gamesmanship and rule-bending in international lineouts than at any other level of the game and the big challenge is to try to outwit your opposite number, either by the use of your own technique or more subtle support play. When you see forwards querying penalty decisions at the lineout it is usually because they want to know exactly what the referee *has* penalised. Let's face it, if he gave a penalty for every offence committed, the ball would never get back into play!

Away from technical emphasis, in the England camp we normally change the lineout calls every season. We made an exception in the two Grand Slam seasons by retaining in 1992 the calls Brian Moore thought up for the previous year. They were so complicated that it took us the first year to work them out! In fact, Brian's lineout calls have always been a bit of a nightmare for poor Mike Teague. Working as he does in the city, Moore has a good head for figures – and invariably comes up with a complicated system involving additions, subtractions, dividing by two and whatever. That is all very well for the university boys, but when you are dealing with a brickie the scientific stuff needs to be toned down a bit. Come to think of it, the calls took me a while to work out too! On our way to Cardiff for the 1991 game against the Welsh, Mike was still asking about the lineout calls in the bus travelling down to the match. We had been working on them for several weeks . . . but he just couldn't fathom out what it was all about!

At the time of writing, no one knows how the new lineout rule will affect the game in the northern hemisphere but I can see referees having problems trying to police it. They face another daunting task in adjudicating the amended law stipulating that a jumper can only use his inside arm for ball-winning, not to work on his opposite number as so many of us do. Apart from all the other lineout offences referees have to judge, most of them are conscious of their obligation to keep the play flowing.

Another rule change I am not sure will work is the one depriving teams taking the ball into contact at ruck and maul situations of the subsequent scrum put-in unless they emerge with possession. The idea of the change seems to be to make players work harder to release the ball as soon as they come into contact. What the IB have failed to acknowledge is that some players are experts at wrapping up the ball and preventing its release. Whereas the emphasis until now has been to keep players on their feet, driving the ball-carrier forward to ensure getting the put-in, the new law will just encourage the opposition to tie in the ball and go to ground. It is open to abuse and I can see occasions when the team driving the ball in will take the law into their own hands out of sheer frustration and because they might lose possession. The rule is really going to need some sympathetic refereeing.

Some of the rule changes make a great deal of sense, like five points for a try, for instance, and players not kicking into touch when the ball is taken back from outside the 22. But others just detract from the skills and principles of the game and it is sad the IB feel it necessary to make so many amendments. The lineout, in particular, is an area enjoyed in its existing form by players and spectators alike. In my opinion it would have been better left alone.

Away from the laws, another contentious problem in the modern game is that of drug abuse. As someone who has no time for players who use steroids and other artificial substances to boost their performance, it came as a huge shock when I was dope tested after one international a couple of years ago . . . and failed! Little did I know it at the time, but the Otrivine nasal spray I was using to cure a persistent breathing problem contained traces of a suspect substance. Questions were asked but fortunately England team doctor Ben Gilfeather, who had himself prescribed the medication, was able to clear the air with the authorities by explaining that I was *not* a drugs cheat and would never entertain anything of the kind. And ever since that day I have made a point of seeing I don't get up anyone's nose again . . . by using a completely different spray.

While I am a great supporter of drugs testing as a concept, when my name came out of the hat as one of the two 'victims' at *four* successive Twickenham internationals, I finally dug my heels in and refused to be tested. On the law of averages that simply was not on . . . and I suspected some sort of conspiracy because they knew that as a policeman it was a safe bet I would be in the clear.

What I didn't know at that time was that the decision had nothing to do with the RFU but was taken at the instigation of the match officials, who select the numbers at random prior to the game. And after some frenetic pleading from various committee men, coupled with veiled threats that refusal could cost me my England place, I finally agreed to go through the torture once more. Peeing into a bottle when you are totally dehydrated can be somewhat challenging. In fact it's not unusual for players to take an hour or more to come up with the required sample. While after-match celebrations are going on in the changing-rooms, the targeted player invariably finds himself stuck in some broom cupboard of a doctor's room with a sample bottle in hand, closely guarded by doctors and officials as he gulps down gallons of liquid in an attempt to speed up events.

Although some South African players have been hitting the head-lines recently over steroid use, it has never been a major problem in this country. There were unsubstantiated rumours a couple of seasons back of suspicious activities by one or two Welsh players, but having said that I have never knowingly come across anyone in this country who used drugs.

I was not surprised, however, to hear during the summer that South African prop Balie Swart had tested positive, along with Eastern Province flanker Elandre van den Berg. I played alongside Swart in Hong Kong earlier this year and even though Afrikaaners do tend to be naturally big, he was absolutely huge – twice the size of Jeff Probyn, in fact. Yet for all the positive testing both men were only suspended briefly before the SARFU's disciplinary committee came up with the ridiculous verdict that they had taken the drugs 'unintentionally'. Since steroids were apparently involved, I find it difficult to believe they did not know what they were doing. In my opinion both players should have faced an immediate two-year ban since using drugs to gain an unfair advantage over players who compete naturally is pure unadulterated cheating.

The worrying thing about South Africa's return to the international fold is that a lot more Springboks than we think could be on steroids and other performance-enhancing drugs. Since the game is effectively semi-professional over there, players want to get bigger, faster and stronger in the least possible time. The higher the stakes, the greater the risk of drug abuse, which in my view is one of the strongest arguments for keeping the game amateur.

It is not only the rules that are changing in rugby. We are rapidly entering a new world in terms of finance and organisation and I am delighted that the players have even managed to drag the RFU into the 20th century! When I first entered the international set-up, the organisation was so antiquated that no one even bothered to tell me I needed a dinner suit! In those days players were expected to pay their wives' travelling expenses and for their hotel rooms prior to the game, which meant that for the first few seasons Sharon never travelled to away matches. Much as she would have liked to have joined the other wives, we simply could not afford it.

Things have improved tenfold since then and the people most responsible for generating Twickenham's massive income are finally being treated properly. Yet, for all that, the RFU still had the cheek to send bills to northern-based England players for flying our wives to London for the double Grand Slam clincher against Wales. I simply couldn't believe it when an invoice for £80 dropped through the letter-box after Sharon and I had returned home to Blackpool. Mind you, it could have been worse because Sharon had a lift down to Twickenham and only flew one way. The bills received by the other northern-based players – Dewi Morris, Nigel Heslop and Martin Hynes – were for twice that amount because their better halves had return tickets! We would have had to pick up the tab too, but for the fact that the Press got wind of it. The subsequent publicity put the RFU under so much pressure that they finally saw the light and we were all told: 'Forget the bills. They are on us.'

Generosity towards the players has never been one of the RFU's greatest attributes. In fact their pettiness over motor expenses actually caused me to change my travel plans to Twickenham. I always used to drive down to matches and squad sessions, claiming the menial 15p a mile allowance at a time when the police paid three times as much! The round trip from Blackpool was 550 miles and the bill to the RFU, just over £80, was scarcely extortionate. Yet I finished up having a running battle with the accounts office over the correct mileage. My claim would perpetually be knocked down and when I queried it I was told they had consulted the RAC and been informed the total mileage was exactly 480 (as the crow flies, no doubt) so that was what I would be reimbursed for. All that fuss over 70 miles, or £10.50 if you prefer. Okay, I said, if they were going to be so petty then in future I would fly down. Do that by all means, replied HQ, that is fine as long as you produce all the relevant receipts. So I adopted a new routine of flying from Manchester which, together with car parking and taxi fares, provided the RFU with a total bill for each trip of around £250. And they never once complained at laying out three times the previous cost!

Having said that, these days England players are probably treated better than any of our home union counterparts. The only expense we still have to meet out of our own pockets is our wives' travel to home games; hence those London flight bills. Some thank-you for two Grand Slams and a World Cup final! Surely it is not asking too much that the people who generate the massive amounts of money Twickenham makes from internationals be given a little bit of special treatment – like having *all* expenses for wives and families reimbursed when they travel to matches.

The game in England has grown out of all recognition in the last few years with Grand Slam and World Cup success generating millions of pounds for the RFU. Since it is the players the people come to watch, it seems only right that they be allowed to benefit from off-the-field activities like sponsorship, personal appearances, writing books and opening supermarkets. I am not advocating direct payment for playing, but whilst the hierarchy quite rightly expect players to be professional in their attitude and commitment, we merely want the chance to take advantage of activities outside the game.

The RFU's argument is that they don't want money taken away from the game. The England players' answer to that is: 'Neither do we, so what's the problem if an international clothing company or sports equipment manufacturer want to pay an individual for wearing and promoting their products?' Gradually we are getting there . . . though it has been a long, slow haul. And when all is said and done we are merely catching up with countries like New Zealand, France, South Africa and Italy, where players have been reaping the rewards for years.

Much has been made of the *Run with the Ball* promotion campaign, and the individual spin-offs each player would get; but the fact is that by the time of writing, eight months after the World Cup, the England players had received just £1,000. That is a just drop in the ocean compared to the grand amounts that were being talked about when our campaign began.

The demands on players in England are increasing and the crunch will come when the Courage League adopts its plan to run the First Division on a home and away basis. It is far too much of a burden to expect amateurs to play 22 or 24 league games, with all the commitment and travelling that entails, and also make themselves available for cup and representative matches. Such a demanding routine, week in, week out, is fraught with pressure and borders on professionalism. Yet that is the total commitment being asked of people whose jobs, after all, lie outside the game.

Don't get me wrong. League rugby itself has proved a marvellous innovation and a breath of fresh air. Instead of going through the motions it has given players a target, something to work towards, and a competitive edge; so much so that down at Preston we now start pre-season training in mid-June! Our leagues are also the envy of the Aussies and New Zealanders, whose club rugby is poor with the emphasis almost entirely on provincial games.

However, one thing that saddens me about the advent of the Courage League has been the consequent demise of the County Championship. Next to playing for England, nothing used to give me more pleasure than turning out for Lancashire. In fact, playing in the Championship-winning side against Warwickshire at Twickenham back in 1988 was one of my most memorable moments. It also used to be a major part of the season's calendar to travel across the Pennines for the Roses clash, which for Yorkshire players like Peter Winterbottom, Rory Underwood, Rob Andrew and indeed Will Carling was a stepping-stone to England recognition.

Constant changes to the County Championship format have reduced it to junior level in recent years . . . and instead we have seen the emphasis switched to the Divisional Championship. Players at top level don't enjoy the divisionals, a fact borne out by the continual failure of the South West to make any impression, even with the combined might of Bath, Gloucester and Bristol at their disposal. And when half the London side are northerners the whole concept becomes a bit of a joke.

With the advent of the league system, Geoff Cooke has a team of assessors watching the best players in England virtually every Saturday. The divisionals provide a chance for them to see the top 60 performing against each other in a series of trial matches away from the club environment; but the feedback I get, and indeed my own view, is that it is an added burden which the players are less than enthusiastic about.

While these games are generally poorly attended, and do not capture the imagination of spectators in the way the County Championship does, playing for a divisional side against a powerful touring nation is somewhat different and stirs the emotions of players and supporters alike. It also gives the likes of the proud northern region the chance to soften up overseas opposition before they go on to meet the national side. No touring side relishes a trip to Cross Green, Otley, where the North have built a reputation for making the most feared of visiting sides look very ordinary.

Although the County Championship must stay, only players from outside the First Division should be eligible. It gives those in the lower leagues the chance to perform at a higher level and for clubs such as Preston, where players can only dream of the dizzy heights of international rugby, a county cap is the goal to aim for and an honour that is treasured and won with intense pride. A prime example in this year's Lancashire side was Paul Grayson from my own club, who went on from the County Championship final to represent England Under-21s. The taste of representative rugby gave him the incentive to move clubs to Second Division Waterloo, with our blessing, to seek further honours.

My North involvement ended abruptly a couple of years ago when chairman Ted Wood informed me by letter that the coaching triumvirate of Dave Robinson, Fran Cotton and Steve Smith had decided to exclude me because they felt I was not committed to the divisional cause. The decision hurt, and not only because the allegation was demonstrably untrue. Since it was a development which could have had repercussions for me at England level, surely I was entitled to the decency of a phone call and explanation, if not a personal hearing.

It seemed that judgement had been passed purely on the fact the North had had a poor season the previous year; and part of the blame for not winning the Divisional Championship was placed squarely – but not fairly – at my feet. I reckoned I had shown total commitment in helping the team to two divisional titles and in fact I had even played at one stage carrying a knee injury. If that wasn't commitment, I don't know what is. I also found it ironic that assistant coach Steve Smith was involved in the decision because whenever I trained with the North at his own club Sale, he was always noticeable by his absence! Since other players managed to travel from all over the region on a Wednesday evening, it made me wonder who was the person showing lack of commitment.

My immediate reaction on hearing the decision was to phone Geoff Cooke, who had been North manager in my early days with the side. My big concern was that my England place might be in jeopardy . . . but while the news came as quite a surprise to him, he assured me I was still very much part of his plans. Unexpectedly presented with extra breathing space, I promptly booked myself in for a minor knee operation I had been needing for ages. In a strange way, the North selectors had done me a favour.

In recent years, England rugby tours have been attracting a Press corps that consists of more than the true rugby correspondents. With increased media awareness of the game, the scene is being invaded by hacks from the non-rugby tabloids whose motives are, I suspect, considerably less honourable. They seem to be looking for more than genuine rugby stories – like players overstepping the mark in some way. It is a totally new concept, and something we just have to learn to live with. We have also started to attract the attentions of the paparazzi – the mercenary band of photographers better known for their intrusive pictures of the Royal Family and film stars. These people don't seem to bother checking accuracy and details, as I discovered to my cost after the last Grand Slam dinner. When the flashlights started popping as I left the Hilton Hotel with RFU players' assistant Ian Lambie, I jokingly put my arm around his wife Julie. Next morning one of the newspapers carried the picture with a caption describing Julie as Mrs Dooley. No one had bothered to ask . . . yet if they had widened the shot a fraction they would have seen Sharon standing right next to us. Needless to say there were a few comments passed afterwards – and not only to myself!

I have had my battles with the Press over the years, but for all that there are a number of journalists I have a great deal of respect for. One of them, Stephen Jones of the *Sunday Times*, found himself on the other side of the fence after Wales beat us in 1989 and subjected to the most embarrassing of post-match episodes I can remember. The England players cringed when the Welsh captain Paul Thorburn chose to use his after-dinner address as a platform for a vitriolic verbal attack on Jones. Instead of venting his displeasure to Steve man to man, he aimed his remarks at the balcony where Jones was sitting, and in front of several hundred guests decribed him as 'the scum of the earth'. Thorburn's comments were out of order. No matter how strong one's feelings, there are correct ways of doing things – and using a public platform to launch personal tirades is not one of them. The comments were not representative either and I told Steve as much later.

Along with Jones I also have great respect for, among others, the *Observer*'s Clem Thomas (who of course was a celebrated Welsh international in his day), *Daily Telegraph* correspondent John Mason and Barry Newcombe of the *Sunday Express*. They work in an unobtrusive way, are true rugby journalists, knowledgeable and informed, and don't poke their noses in where they are not wanted.

The first thing players do on a Sunday morning is to pick up the newspapers and read about their performance the previous day. Obviously they love the good Press when things are going well, and if they are reasonable men they accept criticism when they are playing badly – providing that criticism is constructive. However, there is one lesson I have learnt about the Press over the years. While we both need each other, when the chips are down there is only ever one winner – and it is not the player.

I have been on the end of some scathing media criticism in my time as an England player and in some cases it was justified. However, for certain newspapers it is not enough to have their pound of flesh. Not only do they want to put the knife in; they also want to twist it over and over again. While the top stars are up there on a pedestal waiting to be knocked off, at the end of the day we are all amateurs with a living to earn outside the game. Yet after the Phil Davies affair in 1987 I was hounded by the media to such an extent that I was unable to do the job I am paid for. OK, I had overstepped the mark and was rightly criticised for it. But instead of leaving it at that, neither the Press nor TV knew where to draw the line. They kept at me with such persistence that I had to be taken off the streets and confined to working inside the police station. It was totally out of order, and demonstrates how top Rugby Union players are actually under *more* pressure than full-time professionals. After all, ours is the only game which enables the media to link our sporting careers with our occupations.

It also amazes me that no sooner had he retired from playing than John Jeffrey suddenly appeared on television feigning outrage in a bid to build a new and controversial career. He obviously had his reasons for that verbal attack on me on Scottish TV earlier this year, perhaps to placate the viewing public north of the border, but I find it difficult to believe his words came from the heart. I have every respect for JJ, both as a player and as a person, and I would like to have thought he knew me better than his comments suggested. I only hope that if I finish up providing 'expert' opinions, I have a little more sense and sensitivity than to indulge in such blatant personal attacks.

Another intolerable face of journalism is the way some players are subjected to sustained campaigns of criticism, as Rob Andrew was during the early part of his England career. Had Rob not possessed such strength of character, his confidence could have been totally destroyed and his career ruined.

It was a journalist, Terry Cooper of the Press Association, who first informed me of my one and only offer to turn professional with a Rugby League club. It happened early this year and what a bizarre episode it was! It was clearly a publicity stunt designed to glean maximum exposure since Trafford Borough announced it in the Press fully two weeks before approaching me! Then, seemingly as an afterthought, the following letter arrived at Blackpool police station from company director Allan Sherratt inviting me to discuss a contract to play for the reorganised club for the next two seasons:

> Dear Mr Dooley,
> I write to express our interest in discussing a contract with you to play professional Rugby League for the **1992/1993** and **1993/1994** seasons.
>   Our club is returning to Blackpool to play under the name of Blackpool Gladiators R.L.F.C at Blackpool Arena (formerly Borough Park) commencing this forthcoming August.
>   Whilst we realise that you are currently fully committed to the winning of the Grand Slam with the England Rugby Union team, we felt that you might welcome the opportunity to discuss a mutually beneficial playing arrangement with ourselves.
>   This is a genuine approach and not a simple publicity seeking exercise.
>   I would be grateful if you would let me know whether or not you are interested in taking the matter further.

Trafford were the old Blackpool Borough outfit and they obviously felt my high profile as an England player and the fact I was a local lad might assist them on their return to the town under a new name, Blackpool Gladiators. I did not for one minute take the offer seriously and my comments at the time summed up my feelings. What would I do in a game without lineouts, I asked.

Even though Dick Greenwood worked hard on fitness routines at Preston, I found a marked difference when I was first capped between the pace at club and international level. Over the years my fitness programme has not changed that much – but it has certainly become more refined. And whilst it has been well chronicled that I do much of my training alone, I still concentrate on varying my schedule as much as possible.

When I am in full training I'll do some sort of workout every day. I will put in perhaps four or five full sessions a week, alternating running drills and interval training with weights work. However, if I am playing the following day I tone down my preparation to perhaps a light stretching session in the gym. I attach great importance to stretching and loosening off and spend 20 to 30 minutes on a set sequence of warm-up exercises immediately prior to a game and before all training sessions. After training I'll warm down with another stretch then the day after a match I'll go for a light jog just to loosen off. Having said that, I have never regarded daily training as a compulsory exercise. If I fancy a day off I take one.

Whilst I also find plyometrics useful for improving my leaping ability, speed and dynamism, I don't follow the full routine recommended by England fitness adviser Rex Hazeldine. Plyometrics, which develop explosive power and are used by high jumpers, long jumpers and sprinters, entail repeated bounding exercises off the floor on to boxes and over hurdles, which tend to put stress on knee joints and ligaments. Other lineout specialists like Paul Ackford and Nigel Redman have always utilised the programme to the full. But, conscious of previous injury problems, I avoid those aspects and concentrate instead on the less stressful plyometric exercises – without boxes and hurdles. Certainly my own method of preparation doesn't seem to have served me too badly over the years. Before my knee injury in 1986 I put minimal emphasis on stretching, but I worked out a special routine as part of my rehabilitation programme and have stuck to it ever since. The schedule also included a lot of cycling and swimming.

Suppleness is to my mind crucial to both training and playing, yet there are players who don't bother to warm-up or stretch off at all. Steve Bainbridge was a prime example. Even before the most important of internationals Steve would change and then sit and watch his team-mates going through their various warm-up routines. Then immediately before the game he would get up casually, touch his toes a couple of times . . . and head off with the rest of us into the tunnel.

It took me less than my first 80 minutes of international rugby to realise that I was nowhere near fit enough to compete at that level. Yet a month after my debut against Romania I was a different man – thanks to that training schedule I worked out with my police pal Alan Todd, a fitness fanatic and former fell runner. Before then my attitude was very much the same as that of Dean Richards. Basically I played to keep fit. I tipped the scales at around 18 stone at that time, only four pounds or so more than my optimum playing weight. But I was carrying a considerable amount of flab which certainly would not have passed one of Rex Hazeldine's fat-testing sessions!

Together with Alan, a non-stop flanker who never received the recognition he deserved, I devised a routine which began with a warm-up, then a strenuous workout up and down a two-mile stretch of sand between Blackpool South Shore and St Annes further along the coast. The first leg would consist of endurance work over the sand-dunes. One of us would take the lead and dictate the pace and the other would follow. Then we would go down to the sand flats and head off at three-quarter pace along the beach to St Annes Pier before turning back for Blackpool.

Anybody who has wandered along a north west beach with the rain driving in from the Irish Sea on a wet January day will understand how much self-motivation it took for us to get wrapped up in our training kit and make for those deserted sands. But it was something I was compelled to do in order to compete on equal terms against the French in England's next game. On the way back we would recreate the sort of running required in match conditions, with a variety of short sprints, jogging and three-quarter-pace work, resting briefly in between. On alternate days we would work out in the gymnasium on the seventh floor of Blackpool police station, using a combination of the multi-gym and free weights. Between circuits in the gym we would run up the station's entire eight-storey flight of steps, then walk down – and repeat the exercise as many as seven or eight times. Because of our shift patterns and irregular hours, we would sometimes find ourselves training at one or two o'clock in the morning, which was certainly not conducive to a balanced training schedule.

The programme worked wonders over that initial one-month period, and it was something I utilised over the next few seasons. But once Geoff Cooke joined the England set-up the whole fitness regime improved. He brought in Tom McNab and Rex Hazeldine as advisers, and also introduced fitness testing for the first time. That in itself was an incentive in that it created healthy competition between players to reach new peaks. With the refinement of fitness programmes, training actually became easier in that much of it was mapped out for us . . . particularly in the build-up to the 1991 World Cup. We were given schedules more than 12 months ahead, detailing exactly what we should be doing at given times – when to rest, when to build up the training and at which time of year to peak. Each player was also issued with his own personal ergometer equipment. The rowing machines were on lease to the RFU, and since they were too bulky to keep in the house I took mine to work, where it was put to such good use in the gym – and not only by me. In fact, it was so popular with my colleagues that after I returned it to Twickenham the police invested in one for themselves.

These days I still alternate my training between running, weights and ergometer work, and the beach and police station gym are still integral parts of the programme. But variety is the spice of a successful training schedule and since I am fortunate to live in the country, I also enjoy running along the lanes around my home. The important thing is not to get bored, so I make a point of taking different routes while occasionally I will go down to a running track. I usually run out to a point perhaps two miles away, then concentrate on interval training coming back, alternating between timed sprints, resting, jogging and periods at three-quarter pace. Also, thanks to the management and staff, I was able to make full use during the 1991 World Cup of the gym and facilities at Drake's Fitness Club at the Broughton Park Hotel not far from my home.

In a way, I find training specifically for rugby easier as I get older since my programme these days is more structured and tailored to my needs. But as I approach the end of my playing career I face the same problem as many other sportsmen: I happen to be one of those unfortunate people who really has to watch what he eats. I only have to look at a pint of beer, a plate of chips or a loaf of bread and I can put on half-a-stone. So retirement, for me, will only be the beginning . . .

CHAPTER FIFTEEN

Men for all Seasons

THE England players have never been so much in the public eye as they are today. Our historic achievement in winning back-to-back Grand Slams and reaching the World Cup Final captured the imagination of a loyal public who had waited more than a decade for success on the rugby field. It was the culmination of years of hard work for a squad of players who have become friends as well as team-mates under arguably the most successful regime England have known. While the names and faces of the squad have to some degree become public property, the characters behind the masks are not quite so well known. So, with tongue in cheek and no apologies for insensitivity, I have compiled the following personal dossier as a tribute to the team-mates who provided a silver lining to my international career.

Cockney JASON LEONARD, the baby of the England pack, has been a good young find for England, even if he is strongly rumoured to be a relation of RFU technical administrator Don Rutherford. He seems able to do no wrong in Rutherford's eyes. The young pup has proved very strong in the loose-head position after being brought in to replace the master himself, Paul Rendall. Indeed, it is a measure of the old-stager's respect that Jason is the only player I have known the Judge to take under his wing and pass on tricks of the trade to. One of the fittest members of the England pack, he combines mobility with good handling qualities and defence. He also supports the lineout well and possesses a good temperament which belies his youth. His first cap sent him into such a spin that he actually sat and watched his England kit throughout its debut cycle in the washing machine!

BRIAN MOORE, better known as Cato, the Mad Jap or Pitbull is, of course, a founder member of the David Campese Fan Club. An abrasive little character, you can never shut him up long enough to get a word in edgeways. He doesn't pull punches with his opinions of the opposition and indeed of England ('Nobody likes us but we don't care'). As players' spokesman in the head-to-head with the RFU hierarchy over Player Vision, the England players' limited company, solicitor Brian didn't make too many friends in the committee room at Twickers. Deeply patriotic, he was responsible for introducing a tape of *Jerusalem* and Henry the Fifth's Agincourt speech on to the team bus before the 1991 Grand Slam decider against France. The pinpoint accuracy of his throw-ins is one of the reasons Paul Ackford and myself have been held in such high esteem – after the first 10 minutes of each game, that is. Brian gets so hyped up that the sky's the limit at early lineouts, with throws zooming at least a foot higher than called . . . and Will Carling in the centre almost as likely to take the ball as myself! Ever the showman, Brian is never far away from the camera, and his Oscar-winning amateur dramatics in the players' tunnel at Murrayfield after the World Cup semi-final will live in the memories of the English team for a long time to come. There he was leaning up against the wall with his head in his hands, peering out with a pained and exhausted look on his face . . . and one eye searching for the TV camera.

Captain-of-the-bench JOHN OLVER has been a long-standing member of the squad through the good times and part of England's support team of unsung heroes. A plausible character and practical joker, he has more ruses to escape training sessions than any man I know. Together with the Judge, John has worked wonders to keep morale high – often when things weren't going so well. He usually takes the role in tour courts of Mr X, the undercover and heavily-disguised character who appears for the prosecution, supplying trumped-up allegations and dodgy evidence. Hence the nickname . . . Vermin. With John it's been a matter of right place, wrong time. A hooker in the same mould as Brian, he has generally had to play second fiddle – but when he finally won his first cap against Argentina it was fully deserved. He has spent so long on the bench that it's rumoured that in preparation for his retirement from the international arena he has booked into a private hospital at Northampton for an operation to remove the splinters from his backside.

Anyone unfortunate enough to room with insomniac JEFF PROBYN on tour, should be prepared for a rude awakening. He'll get no more than three hours' sleep when Jeffrey has finished watching the black-and-white late-night Polish movie on television complete with subtitles – because if Probes is not playing with his computer game he'll be tuning in again to children's TV at 6 a.m. An awkward customer both on and off the field, he never likes to lose an argument and will swear black is white, even when he knows he's wrong. He is equally always at odds with his opposite number and I've never met a loose-head who enjoys playing against Jeffrey. He's such an odd shape – no shoulders, no backside and all stomach. Naturally strong in the upper body, apart from his devastating opposition in the scrummage with his low centre of gravity (which some say is illegal), he does a lot of unseen work around the park. He also admits to an intense dislike for training. He picked up the nickname Fibbin after it appeared on his misspelt name-card at a luncheon in Australia.

Noted throughout the squad for his quick-witted repartee, laugh-a-minute PAUL ACKFORD (well maybe one a month if we're lucky!) failed so miserably with his jokes over an airport lounge public address system that he's been known as 'Bernard Manning' ever since. Quite outspoken, he usually took the floor at team meetings . . . and hogged it. Ackers also took the England tour by storm in Australia in 1991 with his hilarious court-jester routine, complete with full costume. In rugby terms, he was simply a world-class player who made life easier for me in our second-row partnership. Normally a four jumper, he accommodated the old-stager by moving to the front in internationals. A great partner and a good friend, he took the dummy I sold him prior to the World Cup Final when we both decided we were retiring after the Australia match. But he landed on his feet with a BBC job as resident TV expert, so look out Starmer-Smith!

I didn't think much of MARTIN BAYFIELD when I first played against him in the divisionals. A big, soft gangling youth, I thought – forgetting that I was once a big, soft gangling youth myself! But he has made me eat my words. Tall players like us will always have a problem with body positions. It takes a lot of hard work and strain on the back, and it was inevitable he would find life difficult following Ackers at the front of the line. But he is prepared to listen to any amount of advice and coped remarkably well in the 1992 Grand Slam season, improving with every game. He will also have learned from his experience Down Under with England B this summer. And don't believe the official line that Martin is only 6ft 10in. Either he's 7ft tall or I'm shrinking . . . because there's definitely more than two inches between our respective heights!

Although PAUL RENDALL has not played for England since the end of the 1990 season, no chapter on my international team-mates would be complete without a mention of the Judge, one of the legendary characters of the squad in recent times. Over his years as head of England's improvised team court on every tour, Paul became so well known by his 'legal' title in general conversation and even outside rugby circles that he would invariably be referred to as the Judge rather than by his own name. In fact it was rumoured that when he was brought from hospital for the pre-match presentation at the World Cup Final following his achilles operation, the Queen said to him 'Hello Judge, how's that leg of yours?' Paul was one of the best lineout support players in the game and seemed to get fitter as he got older.

PETER WINTERBOTTOM is a maverick who has travelled extensively around the world and played in the best company. He has also been able to make the amazing transition from farm labourer to successful city Eurobond dealer. Otherwise known as Strawman, Horseface or Simple, Peter is one of the most respected openside flankers in the game and if I was picking the England team, his would be the first name I would pencil in. We all marvelled at Mick Skinner's tackle on Marc Cecillon in the World Cup, but Wints is every opposing outside half's nightmare – borne out in a 1988 Australia v England game when I saw him cut Michael Lynagh in half and knock him back all of five metres, only to get pulled up for a dangerous tackle. Once criticised for being more of a destroyer than a creator, he worked hard on his game and is now often a crucial link in the England try-scoring chain.

Iron MIKE TEAGUE, or Twelve-Toer, makes Dolly Parton look anorexic in the chest department. A devotee of weights and body-building, he is awe-inspiring when driving forward with the ball in hand. A quiet man with a great sense of humour, Mike's one of the best support players around at number five in the lineout. If he has one weakness it's that he could never understand the signals. So much so that he has been caught many times in team meetings with his trainers and socks off, using his fingers and toes to work out Brian Moore's calls. Mike's nickname stemmed from dressing-room rumours of inter-marriage and inter-breeding down Gloucester way!

If looks were anything to go by, not one member of the opposition would take to the same field as DEAN RICHARDS. With his ambling gait, close-cropped hair, missing front teeth, outsized shorts and socks down around his ankles, Deano looks more like an inmate on day release from Wormwood Scrubs than one of the six police officers who have played for England in recent times – together with myself, Paul Ackford, Nigel Heslop, Mark Linnett and Martin Bayfield. An unassuming, genial character, Dean is more at home with his shotgun and fishing rod, which is exactly how he spent most of the World Cup campaign. Recognised as simply the best No. 8 in the world, the mind boggles to think what he could do if ever he got hooked on training and reached peak fitness.

Tremendously strong, he has an uncanny knack of reading the game way ahead of the rest of us. If he could be criticised for anything it would be his pace. Mind you, Paul Ackford and myself had to concur on one point – that Dean's 'Ben-Hur chariot' lean-on style of scrummaging was like having a breath of fresh air behind us! My abiding memory of touring with him is the faces of fellow travellers at a small provincial airport somewhere in Australia when Dean and his sidekick Dave Egerton decided to give the line of luggage a grand ceremonial escort into the baggage reclaim area. Bored with waiting, they vanished from sight . . . only to reappear amidst the suitcases on the slow-moving conveyor belt, sitting cross-legged with arms folded, dressed in number ones and sporting pith helmets!

MICKY SKINNER is the only member of the squad who could have got away with greeting the Prime Minister on his visit to the England dressing-room after the 1992 Grand Slam match with the words: 'Yo, top man'. And when stark-naked Skins exchanged courtesies with Mr Major, little did the PM realise that the hand he was shaking had moments before been used to dry the Munch's most private possessions! A recent Skinner dinner at Blaydon in the north east confirmed the cult-figure status the people's hero has achieved. The whole of Newcastle seemed to have turned out to pay homage to the Geordie back-row destroyer. If you are in company at an evening function with Mick, keep one eye on the ice-bucket and one on the gateau. You may end up wearing them both. Ever the prankster, there is also a serious side to him. After missing out on England's first Grand Slam and many public warnings from the management regarding his carefree attitude to training and squad life, he got his act together and grasped the opportunity with both hands – playing a full part in the World Cup and 1992 Grand Slam. His flowing locks are never far away from any England try-scorer.

We call RICHARD HILL Duracell because he goes on . . . and on . . . and on. Ever dependable and the most dedicated of trainers, Hilly was criticised at one time for his pass so he responded by working on the speed of his delivery from the base of the scrum. One hundred passes in training per day off both hands is now the norm and these days the pass resembles a tracer bullet, giving Rob and Co. even more space and time. The emphasis on the pass detracted from Richard's natural game of taking on the opposition back row. He was criticised after the World Cup Final for being too predictable . . . hence he lost his place to Dewi Morris for the 1992 Grand Slam campaign. But the two scrum-halves have struck up a great partnership off the field and despite their rivalry have been very supportive of each other. Hilly has also been on the end of some awful spiked lineout ball, courtesy of Paul Ackford and myself, where he collected both ball and opposition pack simultaneously. Yet, hard-nut that he is, he never complained and just got up and on with the job every time. Mind you he'd usually have something to say about it *after* the game. Richard is also the cultural attaché of the England team, with Hill's Tours a renowned part of every overseas trip. Chocolate is one of his main weaknesses, and he will crawl over broken glass for a bowl of chocolate ice cream.

I used to think the only good things to come out of Wales were the roads to England, but that was before I met Colin DEWI MORRIS. The Crickhowell Mute had the same sort of grounding as me in north west junior rugby, where he first made his name at Winnington Park. Proud of his Welsh upbringing, he took some almighty stick from the squad at Cardiff in 1989 when he sang *both* anthems. Speculation still persists in the north that if Dewi had played in the World Cup Final England would have won. Personally I think that sort of talk is unfair both on him and Richard Hill because nobody will ever know the answer. Like Hilly, he showed total dedication by working tirelessly on his pass after being dropped in 1989 amid questions about the weakness of his delivery. He finally won his place back and played a key role in the 1992 Grand Slam success.

ROB ANDREW, or Squeaky (as in clean), is every mature lady's pride and joy. Wouldn't they just love to mother him and polish those shiny, rosy cheeks! He's certainly my great-aunt Margaret's favourite of all the England players. Erratic with his place-kicking in the early days, the best thing Rob did was to hand over the responsibility to Simon Hodgkinson and, latterly, Jon Webb. He came of age on the British Lions tour in 1989, when he arrived in Australia as replacement for injured Paul Dean – and proved he should have been picked in the first place by becoming one of the biggest successes of the series. Rob has an uncanny knack with his pinpoint kicking of keeping his pack going forward – and there's no more encouraging sight when you stand up from a scrum than to see the ball sailing away behind the opposition into touch near the corner flag. He never shies away from the tackle and you won't find a braver stand-off in the world. We go back a long way, having made our England debuts together against Romania in 1985.

JEREMY GUSCOTT is one half of the Jack and Joan double act in the centre with Will Carling – based on *I'm All Right Jack* and *Me Myself I*, by Joan Armatrading. A class player with a touch of arrogance, he came into the squad with an almighty chip on his shoulder, but has settled in to become an important part of the England team. Always unpredictable and very much the individual, even his own team-mates never know what he is going to do next with his electrifying breaks and sudden turn of pace. When not posing on a modelling assignment, Jerry hits a pretty mean golf ball and as a novice was the straightest and longest hitter I've seen.

Old Bum-Chin, WILL CARLING, could have opened his own ladies' lingerie shop after the World Cup given the amount of admirers who inundated him with items from their bottom drawer. I can't understand why they never sent them to Jeff Probyn, Brian Moore or myself. The word is that England's World Cup video was a best-seller for insomniacs who have been flocking to purchase their copy containing Will's speeches during the tournament. They are great bedtime listening. A world-class centre destined for bigger and better things, he stands the ball up well and on occasion is like an extra back-row forward, driving in to add support to rucks and mauls. The skipper is also my tip to captain the British Lions in New Zealand in 1993. Since he insisted he was accepting his OBE on behalf of the team, I've booked my share for the first two weeks in October.

England have lost a colourful character with the retirement of SIMON HALLIDAY. The gentleman of the squad, with never a hair out of place, he was equally at home at centre or wing, and showed great courage in coming back from a crippling leg injury. Brought into the World Cup squad for his defensive qualities, he is known in the trade as Farquhar for his plum-in-the-mouth accent – or more lately Warwick Suite. The latter nickname came when he excelled himself at getting on his high horse with hotel staff. After the ordered snacks failed to arrive before a big game, Simon picked up the phone and boomed out in his best Farquhar voice: 'Warwick Suite here. Send up those sandwiches and coffee, will you?'

RORY UNDERWOOD is never happier than when he gets his nose stuck into the *Daily Telegraph* crossword, though I've never actually seen him fill in a clue. The Wing Commander had to have his fix of the latest puzzle over his breakfast Rice Crispies before training. If Coca Cola ever go bust, the reason will be that teetotaller Rory has stopped imbibing the stuff. He drinks it by the tanker load! A legend in his own lunch-box, he cocked a snook at Geoff Cooke's diet sheet by living on junk food. Naturally very strong and explosive, pound for pound he proved to be the strongest member of the squad in our Portugal training camp a couple of years ago. In a shot putt exercise he put the forwards to shame throwing a 16lb shot higher and further than anybody else. Rory has retired because he wants to become a fighter pilot, looking to fly his planes like he has played his rugby over the years . . . jetting along at ground level at breakneck speed and dumping on the opposition. England will sorely miss him.

NIGEL HESLOP and SIMON HODGKINSON are so renowned for their thriftiness that the safest place in any pub is between them and the bar. There's no danger of getting trampled underfoot by either as they rush to buy a beer. Sloppy's the only man I know who can peel an orange in his pocket, while Hodgy's nickname Ebenezer says it all. Nigel is a fellow-member of the five-man northern crew who have clocked up thousands of BA air miles over the years shuttling between Manchester and Heathrow. He and I go back a long way, well before England, to the annual Lancashire v Merseyside police area finals, which can only be described as lively affairs. A late starter, his sudden elevation to the England side in Argentina took him more by surprise than anybody else. Since then, he has learnt to have confidence in his own ability and has grown from it. Rewarded in his first year with the Grand Slam, he must wonder what all the fuss is about. He was unlucky that Simon Halliday was around at the same time to get the World Cup vote, because there wasn't much in it. Nigel does a cracking impression of Stan Laurel . . . and looks like him too. As for Hodgy, after a disaster in Argentina, he bounced back to break all sorts of records in England's first Grand Slam. A plain-speaking Midlander with a dry sense of humour, his methodical and reliable kicking style has been likened to a perfect golf swing. He's not one of the biggest fullbacks in the world, but makes up for his lack of size with total reliability.

Unlike Mike Teague, weight training is not one of JONATHAN WEBB's favourite pastimes. He did well in Rex Hazeldine's fat tests; in fact I've seen more meat on a jockey's whip. Jon improved out of all recognition after moving from Bristol to Bath and grew in confidence, too. The rest of England can relax when Webby's under the high ball. He's as dependable in defence as he is dangerous coming into the line. His kicking has had to be good since taking over from the maestro, Simon Hodgkinson.

The above players are just a few of the England internationals I have played alongside since making my debut against Romania back in 1985 – but if I was asked to name the *best* possible England side from the 1985–1992 era it would have to be the following – **Jonathan Webb; Rory Underwood, Jeremy Guscott, Will Carling, Simon Halliday, Rob Andrew, Richard Hill; Jason Leonard, Brian Moore, Jeff**

Probyn, Paul Ackford, Yours Truly, Mike Teague, Peter Winterbottom, Dean Richards.

Of course I have also been lucky enough to play with or against virtually all the world's greatest players over the same eight-season period. Picking the top 15 of them is a near-impossible task, so much so that when I sat down to compile a list, leaving out England players, I actually came up with 30 – two for each position. However, with my arm twisted, and given permission to name a rival team to face them, this is my final choice for a World XV – **Serge Blanco (France); John Kirwan (New Zealand), Philippe Sella (France), Tim Horan (Australia), David Campese (Australia); Jonathan Davies (Wales), Nick Farr-Jones (Australia), Steve McDowell (New Zealand), Daniel Dubroca (France), Richard Loe (New Zealand), Gary Whetton (New Zealand), Bob Norster (Wales), Simon Poidevin (Australia), Michael Jones (New Zealand), Wayne Shelford (New Zealand)**.

The team to face them in what would surely be one of the finest all-star spectaculars ever seen would be: **Gavin Hastings (Scotland); Ieuan Evans (Wales), Brendan Mullin (Ireland), Denis Charvet (France), Patrick Lagisquet (France), Michael Lynagh (Australia), Robert Jones (Wales); David Sole (Scotland), Sean Fitzpatrick (New Zealand), Ewan McKenzie (Australia), Chris Gray (Scotland), Steve Cutler (Australia), Willie Ofahengaue (Australia), Finlay Calder (Scotland), Murray Mexted (New Zealand)**.

As for England, I see no reason why the success story cannot continue. Whereas the 1980 Grand Slam team broke up too quickly, heralding a slide in the national team's fortunes, the new dynasty under Geoff Cooke is geared to continuity. Although a number of players have retired or are contemplating hanging up their international boots, the gradual changeover has made it that much easier for newcomers to blend gently into the existing set-up. The B tour to New Zealand this summer has also provided proof that there is no shortage of talent waiting to fill our boots. With Geoff committed to heading the regime until the next World Cup at least, the outlook has never been brighter. I was fortunate enough to have been in at the beginning of the success explosion, and although my first couple of seasons were a chronicle of ups and downs the whole experience has been one of the most enjoyable parts of my life.

Everything seems to have happened to me over the last seven-and-a-half years and it's been a pleasure just to have been part of it.

CHAPTER SIXTEEN

Life with 'im Outdoors

by Sharon Dooley

I KNEW absolutely nothing about rugby when I met Wade in 1978 and I still don't understand the laws properly. I have always thought it would be nice when Wade eventually retires from playing because he will be able to take me to a match and explain the laws himself. But he claims he doesn't know them either!

If the last 12 months are anything to go by, our elder daughter Sophie will be able to clue us both in before too long. At two-and-a-half she can already differentiate between Rugby Union and Rugby League! During the 1991 World Cup she started to question where her Daddy was for the first time. She was still asking the same thing when Wade went out to play in Hong Kong just after baby Sara was born earlier this year. But now she accepts rugby as a legitimate reason for him being away and gets really excited when she sees him on TV. She'll run up to the screen, point him out and announce: 'That's my Daddy.'

Our relationship should really have been a non-starter because of the distance between our respective bases. We worked in different police forces and on different shifts and while I was stationed at Southport, Wade worked and lodged in Blackpool and his home was Warrington. That meant a good 100-mile round trip to see each other. Going down to watch him play at Lancashire Police headquarters at Hutton on a Wednesday afternoon was an ideal opportunity for us to meet after the game. For me it was a case of getting involved in rugby or not seeing him; and with the social life that surrounded the police team, things just took off.

In those early days several of the police players' girlfriends used to meet at matches and as things developed, four or five of the boys married within a couple of years of each other. Looking back on it now, a few of them actually packed in playing within a year or two of getting married. I suspect their wives had something to do with that decision!

I remember a few weeks before our wedding, my mother pointing out to me that as rugby was so obviously part of Wade's life I was going to have to accept it as a major part of mine. I told her that the only time I would complain about it taking up so much of his time was if he ever purposely shut me out of it. That situation has never arisen in 12 years of marriage.

We didn't even have a honeymoon because of rugby. The Wednesday after our wedding Wade was playing for the police in the quarter-final of the Police Athletic Association Cup at Hutton against the Royal Ulster Constabulary. I suppose I should have realised then that we would spend our life together eating, sleeping and breathing rugby.

I remember one little incident in our first year which I think many rugby players' wives will identify with. One Saturday, Wade's idea of my post-match involvement was to ask me before playing for Hoppers if I would make a curry for supper as he was bringing a couple of the boys home after the game. 'Of course I will,' I said, and proceeded to spend the afternoon preparing a very large pot of curry for three hungry rugby players. In reality there was probably enough for six to eight normal people.

At midnight I received a phone call from Wade, who sounded as though he was enjoying himself, saying that they had called at the home of one of the boys' uncles, who was celebrating his 50th birthday. I found out later that his aunt looked on horrified to see the three of them go across the buffet table like a plague of locusts.

'What about this curry you asked me to make? What am I going to do with it all?' I said, bearing in mind we didn't possess a freezer at that time. 'Don't worry, I'll eat it,' replied Wade. 'You certainly will,' I retorted, 'because I'm not going to cook another thing until it's all gone.' Not surprisingly, his two pals didn't show their faces either, so Wade had to eat the lot on his own over the next two days. Needless to say I never had the same problem again.

In the early years of our marriage the thought of Wade playing at international level never crossed our minds. That day he was first called up by England came utterly out of the blue. It hadn't even figured in our wildest dreams. In fact it didn't even feature in our lives as an ambition. All Wade wanted to do was get his county cap for Lancashire, that was his big rugby dream. It was a well-known fact locally that it was effectively a closed shop; if you didn't play for one of the 'big five' of

Orrell, Waterloo, Fylde, Sale and Vale of Lune you had no chance. When the call finally came I was convinced it had something to do with the fact Wade had done some training with the England squad at Dick Greenwood's invitation. Suddenly the powers-that-be seemed to realise he existed . . . and lo and behold along came that cap he had always cherished.

I remember Wade's first international game being surrounded with confusion as I had found out at the last minute that there was a players' ladies' dinner after the match, and that it was a formal affair. Wade had at least met the rest of the team at training. I didn't know anybody and as our dinner is always separate from the players', I didn't even have the support of my man. However, I needn't have worried as Gary Pearce's wife Sue took me under her wing, a role I was to perform myself in later years as a 'veteran' of the England wives' club. With the RFU, you always know when you've been around a long time; it's when the committee ladies remember you and your children's first names!

Wade used to suffer badly with pre-match nerves but it was only in his second season with England that I realised it. He is normally very placid but in the days leading up to an international there used to be no pleasing him. The slightest thing would get his back up and he was hard work. To be honest I was glad to see the back of him! Then it suddenly dawned on me that he was *always* this way before going off to join the squad. Once they had met and had a training session, he would phone me and he'd be back to his same old easy-going self.

Over the years Wade has had his ups and down on the rugby field and some of the Press reaction has left a nasty taste for both of us. Had he been a plumber and not a policeman, I am convinced the media would not have made half as much of the controversial moments as they have done. The publicity seems to stem from the fact he is a policeman and as such is expected to be whiter than white. Even the faintest speck of grey is unforgivable – and heaven help him if he reacts like a normal human being!

More than five years after it happened, they still keep raking up the 1987 Cardiff game and the unfortunate incident with Phil Davies. Would that happen but for the fact Wade is in the police force? The Press have created an image of Wade that in reality doesn't exist. They portray him as a gross, mean, raw-meat-eating thug who doesn't give a damn about anyone. No wonder when we attend functions members of the public remark to me how surprised they are that he is such a pleasant, mild-mannered, laid-back kind of guy. They have obviously been reading the tabloids.

At the time of that Cardiff saga I was at home with flu, and I saw the action on TV without fully realising what had happened. Wade telephoned me after the match, obviously concerned, but it was only when we watched the game together after he came home that the events of that day were fully brought home to me. On the following Monday a reporter from the *Daily Express* prowled around our village trying to dig up a tasty story. However, he didn't have any success and was eventually seen off by the wife of one of our local farmers. It was strange, but having found out only pleasant things about Wade, not a word appeared in print. After all, it would have ruined the image they had already portrayed in the paper.

During Wade's early England career we took a lot of notice of the Press. With time, however, we have learnt to pick and choose. These days we ignore the sensation-mongers and stick to reading the true sports writers. There is a standing joke among some of the tabloids that the Dooleys have a list next to the telephone of acceptable and unacceptable journalists. The list is now actually in my head – and it all goes back to the Cardiff affair. I always answer the phone and usually manage to beat them off verbally with a big stick. I can sometimes hear the groans of disappointment when a journalist hears my voice at the other end – and certain ones know that they are on a non-starter.

When Wade started going on tours in the summer people used to ask how on earth I put up with him being away for so long. It is something I have become used to over the last few years since he has been away with either England or the British Lions for six out of the last seven summers. From a purely selfish point of view, though, the first couple of weeks after he left for a tour were wonderful! Suddenly all I had to think about was myself. There was no longer any need to work out my menus days ahead to compensate for Wade's work, training and playing routines. I didn't have to worry whether he had a clean shirt or if his kit was clean. The washing basket was empty, there was no ironing pile and I didn't have to cook a meal every night. But the novelty soon wore off.

The world is a small place with a telephone, however, and I have been lucky enough to travel the world through Wade. He has always made a point of phoning to tell me about all the exotic places he has been to; and when he got back he would spoil me silly with beautiful gifts.

I don't think that England rugby tours are events for wives. In fact

I can't think of anything worse than 'wives on tour'. They are in danger of becoming a burden and a hindrance and besides, if I was going to spend a fortune and use my limited annual leave from work to travel to the likes of Australia and Fiji or Argentina, I would want to spend all my time with my man – not traipsing around the country with 20-odd others as well. Despite what some colleagues think back at work, when the squad are on tour they train very hard in order to put in perfect performances on the rugby field. After all, our 'friends' the gentlemen of the Press will crucify them if they don't come up to standard! Due to the on-going pressures of international rugby, and especially over the last couple of years, our private and personal time together as a family has become even more precious. Wives on tour? No, thank you. I'm not that much of a social animal.

There have been some amusing moments during my time as a member of the England wives and girlfriends club, but few more hilarious than when one of Wade's colleagues, Blackpool CID inspector Paul Buschini, turned up at one of England's after-match dinners at the Hilton.

Since the RFU actively discourage gatecrashers, Paul, a typical prop forward who was in the cadets with Wade and plays for both the divisional police team and for Fleetwood, was 'smuggled' into the function along with two or three other colleagues. Wearing Wade's dinner jacket and Dean Richards's bow-tie in conjunction with his own bush-cotton check shirt, blue corduroy trousers and crepe-soled hush-puppies, he cut a fine dash on the dance floor. From his square build and short neck, there's no mistaking Paul is a prop and he had me in stitches as he led me around the dance-floor wearing a jacket which came virtually down to his knees with the sleeves rolled back . . . twice.

Whilst dancing with such a strangely-attired partner was somewhat embarrassing, I also managed to have the last laugh on Paul. RFU committee man Sir Michael Knight, a charming gentleman who at the time happened to be an Air Vice Marshal, subsequently asked me to dance and when he returned me courteously to the company of my strangely-dressed friends, I introduced him to Paul without mentioning his title. "Ere, what d'you do, then?' demanded the inspector in his broad Lancashire accent. 'I'm in the RAF, actually,' replied the Air Vice Marshal with a wry smile. 'You'll know our kid then,' bellowed Paul. 'He's in the Raff up at Lossiemouth.' If anyone's career was destined never to take off, it was Paul's brother-in-law's!

When I returned to work on the Monday Paul was still full of the occasion . . . until I told him with great amusement who Sir Michael really was. You should have seen his jaw hit the floor!

For some reason, folk are always fascinated by the amount of food that tall or large men consume. For his frame and size Wade doesn't eat as much as one would assume. He has always been particular about *what* he eats – and that goes back to the days before the RFU brought in their specialised diet and training programmes. While the England diet sheet must have been a real culture shock for some of the players, it was basically what Wade was eating, anyway. In fact I could have written it for them!

He eats very little red meat, keeping mainly to chicken and fish. However, he is rather partial to the odd chilli. I bought a wok some years ago and it was probably one of my better investments as I tend to stir-fry quite a lot of our food these days. Wade has always been very keen on veggies and especially salad, which I am told is unusual for a man. We tend to have a side-salad with virtually every meal, whatever it is. I can't write about food without mentioning John, our friendly local greengrocer, whose eyes flash pound-signs of delight whenever I enter the shop as I spend on average £30 a week just on fruit and veg. Not bad considering there are only two adults and a toddler consuming it!

Wade's great weakness, though, is bread and when we were first married it was nothing for him to eat a full loaf or more every day. I think that had a lot to do with the guest house in which he had lodged. There was always plenty of bread on the table with every meal. However, he now eats only wholemeal or granary bread – and in more moderate quantities. Of course, he also loves chips but he's lucky if I serve them up five times a year. They come into the 'naughty but nice' category.

The RFU have come further out of the dark ages this last seven years than in the previous 70. When Wade first became involved with the England team, players' ladies were scarcely acknowledged, apart from an after-match dinner – but now we are actually informed about match and tour details. During Sandy Sanders' presidency in 1989–90 a precedent was set that the RFU would pay for wives and girlfriends to travel to away games. During the 1991 World Cup we spent a lovely weekend with the boys in Jersey before the quarter-final in Paris and again a very pleasant few days, kids and all, in Grantham prior to the final.

If anyone had told me back in 1985 that I would be part of such excitement, so much travelling and such wonderful sporting success over the next seven years I would never have believed them. And to crown it all Wade and I, along with other members of England's double Grand Slam team, were among 1,500 guests at the Queen's garden party this July to salute the country's sporting champions over her 40-year reign.

To be there in person at Buckingham Palace in the presence of Her Majesty, Prince Philip and Prince Edward, marvelling at the splendour as we walked around the Royal Family's private gardens, was just a dream come true.

England's Towering Presence

by Paul Ackford

This article is reprinted with the kind permission of the *Observer*.
It first appeared on 1 March 1992.

AT all levels of rugby, forwards tend to congregate at the back of the team bus in an attempt to mirror the physical proximity and camaraderie they show on the field. The All Blacks, when they are on tour, have ritualised this behaviour and challengers for the back seat have to fight their passage down the bus to earn their right to stay. Occasionally, these battles have resulted in broken bones and stitches, and on one infamous occasion this caused a player to withdraw from an international.

Next Saturday, as the England bus makes its short journey from the team's Richmond hotel to Twickenham, Wade Dooley, on the occasion of his fiftieth cap, will be sitting on the extreme right of the back row. He has occupied that seat for as long as I have known him. In fact, while it allows him more leg room it also underlines the respect in which he is held.

Another indicator of esteem in this England squad is the amount of stick you receive. Wade gets more than his fair share. Once, in an airport transit lounge, he sidled up to Brian Moore, who was reading a novel, and innocently asked him what page he was on. John Olver, the substitute hooker, overheard this innocuous question and Wade was rechristened 'Boring Bob'.

He is a highly organised individual whose tidiness is legendary. Most hotel rooms on tour resemble the aftermath of a natural disaster; Wade's is always pristine, a chambermaid's dream. During a players' mock court session, 'Judge' Paul Rendall accused him of ironing the curtains in his room during an idle moment. Needless to say, the verdict was guilty.

Not only has he reigned supreme in aerial combat, he is also a very effective scrummager. Shrewd judges have expressed admiration for the scrummaging abilities of Jeff Probyn. Rightly so, but Jeff has always acknowledged the help he has received over the years from Wade. Occasionally, however good he is, a prop will get himself in a bit of a tangle and will have to sit on the shoulder of his second row hoping that together they can soak up the pressure. Wade has this ability in his armoury.

During his career, Wade has been centre stage in some controversial incidents. In Cardiff in 1987, he was involved in that notoriously ill-tempered match when Phil Davies had his cheekbone broken by a punch. More recently against Scotland, an off-the-ball incident with Doddie Weir attracted unwelcome publicity. Yet he is not a violent man, or player. He won't shy away from confrontation, but he won't seek it either.

My favourite memory of the big man comes from the Lions tour of Australia in 1989. Australia had selected Stephen Cutler and Bill Campbell in their second row for the first Test. The Lions went into the match with myself and Robert Norster as the first-choice pairing. Norster was the undisputed lineout king of Europe and the one player who had continually got the better of Wade in their personal battles.

It was a difficult time for Wade. He had been playing well in the Wednesday team, captained by Donal Lenihan and was a proud member of Donal's Doughnuts, as they liked to be called. However, the manage-ment team, possibly unduly influenced by Clive Rowlands, had plumped for Norster. Not to be chosen was bad enough, but to have missed out to Bob was a double blow. I was close to him on that tour and he never uttered a word of complaint. He never resorted to back-stabbing, he just trained hard and got on with the tour.

We lost that first Test and Wade was selected for the next two, which the Lions won, and he was finally able to exorcise the ghost of Norster. The dignity with which he handled the experience was very special.

Wade has become indispensable to England's fortunes. When England toured Australia and Fiji last summer, he missed both Tests because of a broken bone in his hand. During one of the early provincial games, as he so poetically expressed it, Sam Scott-Young's head had collided with his hand. As a result, I played with Martin Bayfield in the Australia Test and suffered the ignominy of being thoroughly outplayed in the tight and loose. That's not a criticism of Martin. He actually won more ball than I did; it's just an indication of how much Wade was missed. Five months later in the World Cup final, against virtually the same Australian pack, with Wade fit again, we murdered them.

If I were to stretch a point, Wade's original absence might have cost us the final because our ultimately futile, expansive approach was forged as a direct result of our previous humiliation and our new respect for the Aussie pack. Sam Scott-Young has never used his head to better effect.

What makes Wade so special is his presence. Sure, he is 6ft 8in and 17st 10lb but there are other players in first-class rugby as big. Unusually, he actually plays his weight. He is a conscientious trainer – there is no truth in the rumours that you can time his sprints with a sun dial – and he is disciplined in his eating habits. Wade was eating pasta, fish, skinless chicken and fruit salad long before they became *de rigueur* for budding internationals. Mind you, he has never quite got the hang of the white wine.

As a person he is conservative, content with his own company, and emphatically his own man. He is one of the few players able to challenge the authority of the management team and get away with it. He does what he wants when he wants. He dominates opponents physically and psychologically. The ultimate respect in international terms is when other nations evolve their tactics to avoid confrontation in key areas where they are patently less effective. Both Scotland and France in the past have conceded the middle of the lineout by trying anything to avoid the head-to-head challenge.

Career Statistics

WADE DOOLEY'S international career began on January 5 1985, when he made his debut for England against Romania at Twickenham. The England line-up that day included just three players who were to survive to play in the 1991 World Cup Final – Rob Andrew, Rory Underwood and, of course, Wade himself. The England team that faced the Romanians was: Nick Stringer, Simon Smith, Kevin Simms, Paul Dodge (capt.), Rory Underwood, Rob Andrew, Richard Harding; Phil Blakeway, Steve Brain, Gary Pearce, John Orwin, Wade Dooley, Jon Hall, David Cooke and Bob Hesford.

Dooley's full international record, up to and including his 50th cap, is a follows:

1985
v Romania (Twickenham). Won 22-15.
v France (Twickenham). Drew 9-9.
v Ireland (Dublin). Lost 7-10.
v Scotland (Twickenham). Won 10-7.
v Wales (Cardiff). Lost 15-24.
v New Zealand (Wellington). Lost 15-42
(came on as replacement for injured Orwin).

1986
v Wales (Twickenham). Won 21-18.
v Scotland (Murrayfield). Lost 6-33.
v Ireland (Twickenham). Won 25-20.
v France (Paris). Lost 10-29.

1987
v France (Twickenham). Lost 15-19.
v Wales (Cardiff). Lost 12-19.

1987 World Cup
v Australia (Sydney). Lost 6-19.
v USA (Sydney). Won 34-6.
v Wales (Brisbane). Lost 3-16.

1988
v France (Paris). Lost 9-10.
v Wales (Twickenham). Lost 3-11.
v Scotland (Murrayfield). Won 9-6.
v Ireland (Twickenham). Won 35-3.
v Ireland (Dublin). Won 21-10 (Millennium match).
v Australia (Brisbane). Lost 16-22.
v Australia (Sydney). Lost 8-28.
v Fiji (Suva). Won 25-12.
v Australia (Twickenham). Won 28-19.

1989
v Scotland (Twickenham). Drew 12-12.
v Ireland (Dublin). Won 16-3.
v France (Twickenham). Won 11-0.
v Wales (Cardiff). Lost 12-9.
v Romania (Bucharest). Won 58-3.
v Fiji (Twickenham). Won 58-23.

1990
v Ireland (Twickenham). Won 23-0.
v France (Paris). Won 26-7.
v Wales (Twickenham). Won 34-6.
v Scotland (Murrayfield). Lost 7-13.
v Argentina (Buenos Aires, First Test). Won 25-12.
v Argentina (Buenos Aires, Second Test). Lost 13-15.
v Argentina (Twickenham). Won 51-0.

1991
v Wales (Cardiff). Won 25-6.
v Scotland (Twickenham). Won 21-12.
v Ireland (Dublin). Won 16-7.
v France (Twickenham). Won 21-19.

1991 World Cup
v New Zealand (Twickenham). Lost 12-18.
v USA (Twickenham). Won 37-9.
v France (Paris – quarter-final). Won 19-10.
v Scotland (Murrayfield – semi-final). Won 9-6.
v Australia (Twickenham – final). Lost 6-12.

1992
v Scotland (Murrayfield). Won 25-9.
v Ireland (Twickenham). Won 38-9.
v France (Paris). Won 31-13.
v Wales (Twickenham). Won 24-0.

Career England record – 50 caps, won 30, drawn 2, lost 18. In those games, Wade scored three tries, against France in 1986, USA in the 1987 World Cup and Wales on his 50th appearance.

BRITISH LIONS TOUR 1989
v Australia (Brisbane – Second Test). Won 19-10.
v Australia (Sydney – Third Test) Won 19-18.